THE
STEPHEN YAN
SEAFOOD WOKBOOK

KEY PORTER BOOKS

Canadian Cataloguing in Publication Data

Yan, Stephen.
  Stephen Yan's seafood wokbook

Includes index.
ISBN 0-919493-87-4

1. Wok cookery. 2. Cookery (Seafood). 3. Cookery (Fish). 4. Cookery, Chinese.
I. Title.

TX747.Y36 1986   641.6'9   C86-093533-7

Key Porter Books Limited
70 The Esplanade
Toronto, Ontario
Canada M5E 1R2

Distributed in the United States of America by National Book Network, Inc.

Photography: Derik Murray
Photo Prop Co-ordinator: Rob Scott
Cover Design: Raymond Mah, Signals Design Group
Typesetting: Computer Composition of Canada, Inc.
Printed and bound in Canada

94 95 96 97 98 6 5 4 3 2

Cover: Ginger Lobster, page 90
      Prawns with Vegetables, page 123
      Steamed Trout, page 64

Contents

Wok Cooking

Why Wok?

Seafood has many characteristics in common with wok cooking.

1. It is convenient. Seafood is available in many forms – fresh, frozen or canned; in deboned, ready-to-cook fillets, and in frozen steak portions and nuggets.

2. Seafood is versatile. It can be prepared in a variety of ways – stir-frying, deep-frying, steaming, and in stews and soups.

3. Seafood cookery is fast. With today's hectic pace, speed is essential. Wok cooking is quick but still offers creativity and fun. The delicate texture of seafood is usually very sensitive to heat, and so requires very quick cooking to retain its original flavor. Unlike most meat, over-cooked seafood will lose its flavor.

4. Seafood is also nutritious. Wok cooking is well known for its incomparable ability to preserve nutritional value. Seafood is wholesome and nutritious – rich in protein, vitamins and minerals – but low in calories. It is recommended for dieters who love to eat well without gaining weight. The flesh is light and easily digestible. With growing health-consciousness, seafood has gained a more popular place in today's diet.

5. Seafood is abundant. It is available commercially or from sport fishing, and from fresh or salt water. This economical food comes in many varieties, providing a wide range of opportunities for creativity and enjoyment.

6. Finally, seafood is popular. With more advanced freezing methods and modern technology, exotic species of seafood can be stored and distributed more widely than ever before. White fish will keep for up to six months in a freezer and oily fish up to two months. And foreign travel has enhanced the knowledge of these delicacies from the water, as holidaymakers bring back memories of interesting and exotic seafood dishes and want to recreate them at home.

Seafood is as compatible with wok cooking as a key is to its lock; together, they open the door to a new way to enjoy delicacies from the water. Why wok . . . Why not?

Tips for Successful Wok Cooking

Planning

Consider your own ability and do not plan for more dishes than you can handle. Choose a few dishes that can be cooked ahead of time and pick only one last-minute dish for your menu.

Preparation

Check the ingredient list and assemble all the ingredients in one place, preferably on a large tray near the stove. Preparation takes more time than the actual cooking, so allow time to prepare all ingredients and have them ready before you begin to cook. Marination should be done ahead of time.

Cooking

Study the recipe before cooking. The skillet or wok must be hot. Use high heat unless specified otherwise. Prepare rice or noodle dishes first; cook vegetable dishes last. When food is being cooked with a lid, *do not* take the lid off until the time is up. If steam pressure is lost, the food will take a longer time to cook. Cook quickly and serve immediately.

Menu Planning

In this book, recipes do not indicate the number of servings, for this depends upon the size of your group and the number of dishes served. With 4 to 6 people, a sufficient traditional Chinese menu should consist of soup, rice, 1 vegetable dish and 3 meat or seafood dishes. For every additional 2 people, another meat or seafood dish should be added. If you are serving a traditional Chinese meal, a good rule of thumb is to prepare soup, rice or noodles, and 1 main course dish per person. If you want to use only 1 wok seafood dish, you should complement it with soup, salad, rice or noodles and a vegetable for a family of 4 to 6 people.

Dishes should be selected for contrast and diversity. When one is spicy, another one should be bland; if one is meaty, another should have more vegetables; when there is one shellfish dish, others should have other kinds of seafood; when a filling dish like steamed rice is planned, avoid another filling dish like chow mein or fried rice. Include only one last-minute stir-fry dish per menu; the rest should be dishes that can be prepared ahead of time.

Basic Utensils for Wok Cooking

The Wok

The wok is a concave metal pan that looks like a salad bowl. A wok with a 14" diameter is sufficient for cooking for 2 to 15 people. Flat-bottomed woks can sit directly on top of the electric burner and conduct heat quickly. They are especially good for a smooth-topped stove. They require more oil for cooking, burn food more easily, cannot be tilted to the side for cooking and hinder tossing of ingredients. Round-bottomed woks are what we recommend. They require less oil in cooking and have no corners to hinder the turning or removal of food. They also conduct heat more effectively. They require a metal collar or base and can be used for gas, electric or open-fire cooking. They were originally designed by the Chinese thousands of years ago and are still used today.

A spun-steel wok requires scrubbing and seasoning. It must be completely dry after use, or it will rust. A stainless steel wok with copper bottom is popular in Western kitchens because it never requires seasoning or gets rusty. Usually it is dishwasher proof and requires minimal care. A teflon-coated wok is not recommended because teflon hinders heat conduction. You cannot stir-fry with a metal spatula because of damage to the teflon. Electric woks are not recommended because they are less flexible; they cannot be used on gas ranges, or be tilted during cooking. They are very expensive but less efficient.

The Wok Base

The wok base for an electric stove is usually made with steel. It sits in the inside circumference of the electric burner and should not cover the chrome ring of the stove, because the reflection of the high heat used in wok cooking will discolor the stove's enamel. It should have 3 holes on the side to prevent over-heating. For a gas stove the base is larger, higher and has more holes so that air can get in to assist the fire combustion.

The Wok Cover

A 13" cover fits a 14" wok. The wok cover helps to build up steam pressure, particularly in vegetable cooking and meat stewing.

The Cleaver

A very versatile and indispensable item. Its broad blade allows uniform cutting and thin slicing. It can also be used for shredding, dicing, peeling and slivering. It replaces a whole battery of knives used in an average Western kitchen. Carbon steel cleavers rust easily if not properly dried; stainless steel cleavers are also available.

The Chinese Spatula

This metal spatula is curved to fit a round wok. It is used for stirring and turning ingredients to prevent burning.

The How-Tos of Wok Cooking with Seafood

How to Use the Recipes in This Book

The recipes in this book have been developed with four basic principles in mind.
1. Easy preparation. Every dish requires a total preparation time of less than an hour and is very easy to make. As long as there is a basic knowledge of ordinary cooking and an interest in learning wok cooking, success is guaranteed.
2. A systematic procedure. Every recipe includes step-by-step instructions in simple form. This cookbook uses the same professional systematic approach practiced in restaurant cooking. Our method has been proven successful both in our cooking classes as well as in public demonstrations across North America.
3. Flexibility and versatility. Ingredients can be altered in quantity or substituted altogether without changing the result drastically. The book simply demonstrates the wok technique without dictating exact measurements. Use your creativity and imagination – our simple technique will allow you to wok up a storm.
4. Availability of ingredients. The aim of this book is to help you to enjoy wok cooking with seafood using ingredients most commonly found in your market. Substitutions can be used if certain ingredients are not available. For example, salt can be used to replace soy sauce, tapioca starch can be used for cornstarch, or just ordinary water can be used to replace soup stock. When cooking wine is called for, use any kind of cooking wine or dry sherry; use any kind of vegetable oil for cooking. This book allows you to wok any way you want, as long as you follow the step-by-step instructions. Our grandmothers seldom tied themselves down with exact ingredients, so relax and enjoy yourself as you wok. It's not what you wok with, it's how you wok that counts.

How to Season Spun-Steel Woks

1. Scour the inside with a scouring pad, soap and water for about 5 minutes. Rinse and dry well with a paper towel.
2. Smear oil on the inside surface.
3. Heat over high heat until wok becomes discolored. Tilt wok for even seasoning. The discoloration indicates that the wok has been seasoned.
4. After use, the wok should be washed immediately and dried by putting it back on the cooling stove. The remaining heat will provide extra dryness.

Alternatively, you can use the following method:

1. Wash the wok with a scouring pad, rinse and dry with a paper towel.
2. Oil the whole wok, inside and out.
3. Put wok in the oven at 230°C (450°F) for 30 minutes. The whole wok will turn black. This discoloration indicates that the entire wok has been seasoned.

How to Heat the Wok

1. Place wok in its ring over the burner and turn heat to its highest setting. Heat wok until very hot, about 15 to 30 seconds. A drop of water in the wok should sizzle and evaporate instantly when the wok is hot enough.
2. Add 2 Tbsp. oil in a swirling motion.
3. Still over the highest setting, heat oil until very hot (about 190°C or 375°F), about 30 seconds.
4. When oil is hot, start cooking.

How to Stir-Fry

1. Prepare all ingredients and assemble beside stove.
2. Heat wok and oil as described above.
3. Add ingredients as recipe requires, stirring and tossing them briskly with a spatula.

How to Deep-Fry

You can use your electric deep-fryer if you like, but the traditional Chinese method is described below.

1. Pour about 2 cups oil in wok.
2. Using the highest setting, heat the oil. When the oil ripples and smokes, use a bamboo chopstick to test the temperature. If bubbles form around the chopstick, then the oil is hot enough for deep-frying (about 180°C or 350°F). Reduce heat but maintain a constant temperature. If it is too hot, excessive smoke will shoot up; add extra oil to cool it down before you begin to fry.

How to Steam Seafood

1. Place a heat-proof bowl or pyrex bowl upside down on the bottom of a wok.
2. Pour hot water into the wok but do not allow water to cover the bowl.
3. Arrange food on a heat-proof plate and then place on the bowl.
4. Cover with a round lid. Roll up a wet towel and place it around the edge of the cover.
5. Always use high heat and steam continuously, without taking the cover off until food is done.
6. As a rule of thumb, steam fish for 10 minutes per pound.

Alternatively, you can use this traditional Chinese method.

1. Arrange 2 pairs of bamboo chopsticks in a tick-tack-toe pattern in the wok.
2. Pour hot water into the wok until the water is just below the chopsticks.
3. Arrange food on a heat-proof plate and then place on chopsticks.
4. Cover with a round lid. Roll up a wet towel and place it around the edge of the cover.
5. Always use high heat and steam continuously, without taking the cover off until food is done.

How to Buy and Prepare Fresh Seafood

How to Buy Fresh Fish

Look for the following 5 features when buying fresh fish:

1. Eyes should be bright, clear, shiny and full.
2. Scales should be full and shiny and should cling tightly together.
3. Flesh should be firm and bouncy to the touch.
4. Smell should be fresh and not too strong.
5. Gills should be red and free from mucus.

How to Store Fish

For refrigeration

1. Wash whole fish in cold water and dry on paper towel immediately.
2. Wrap tightly in aluminum foil.
3. Store in refrigerator.
4. Use as soon as possible.
5. Store for no longer than 4 days.

For freezing

1. Wrap or rewrap store-packaged product tightly in heavy aluminum foil and plastic freezer bags or place in an airtight plastic container.
2. Store at −18°C (0°F) or lower.
3. Keep fatty species like salmon, mackerel, herring and lake trout for no longer than 2 months.
4. Keep lean species like sole, perch and smelts for no longer than 6 months.

How to Prepare a Whole Fish

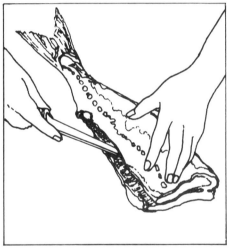

1. Wrap a small piece of wet towel around the tail and hold tail with one hand. Use the back of a cleaver and run it at a 45° angle from the tail to the head of the fish. It's best to do this in a kitchen sink and under cold running water to avoid messiness. Repeat until clean.

2. Use a sharp cleaver or knife and slit the abdomen of the fish to the gills. Remove and discard the gills and the entrails.

3. Chop off the fins. Wash fish under cold running water and drain.

How to Fillet a Fish

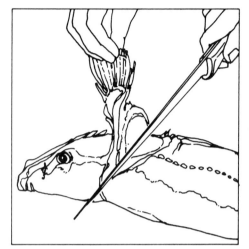

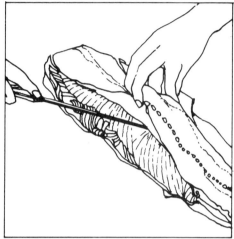

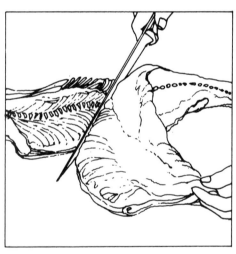

1. Remove the head by cutting it off around the base of the gills. Bend the spinal bones back and forth a few times to break off the head.

2. Using a thin, narrow knife, slit the fish along the spine and slide the blade along one side of the back bone and over the ribs from gills to tail. Hold the fillet as you cut it.

3. Remove the fillet and repeat the same procedure on the opposite side.

How to Buy a Live Crab

Watch for the following features when buying live crab:

1. The crab should be lively and responsive when touched.
2. The eyes should be bright, full and moving.
3. Use your thumb and finger to pinch the back legs; they should be hard and full.

How to Prepare a Live Crab

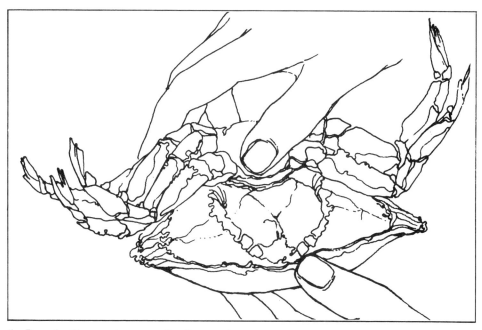

1. Pour boiling water over the live crab.
2. Pull off top shell; remove the "apron" underneath and the gills.

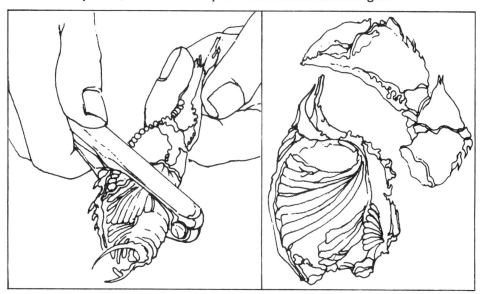

3. Break off the claws and crack the shell with a cleaver or a nutcracker.
4. Cut the body in half and cut the halves into pieces. Legs can be left on the body or be cut off.

How to Shop for Live Lobster

Lobster should be purchased live; if they die before use they should be discarded. The best size is 750 g to 1 kg (1½ to 2 lb.), which will serve 4 people. Watch for the following 6 features when buying lobster:

1. The lobster should be lively and clawing actively.
2. Both claws should be complete.
3. The eyes should be bright, shiny, full and not sunken.
4. The part of the head that is near the body should be firm to the touch.
5. When the lobster is picked up, its tail should move actively.
6. The male lobster has a pair of hard legs immediately below the head, whilst the female has softer ones.

How to Prepare a Live Lobster

There are two ways to prepare a live lobster. One is the boiling method, which is used when cooked meat is required. Simply cook the lobster in a large container filled with boiling water and ¼ cup (60 mL) of salt; boil for 10 minutes for a 1 to 2 lb. (750 g to 1 kg) lobster. This is considered the humane way to kill a live lobster, but it will never give you the nice texture of a good live lobster. When you want roast beef, the meat is never boiled before you roast it; the same principle applies to lobster and crab.

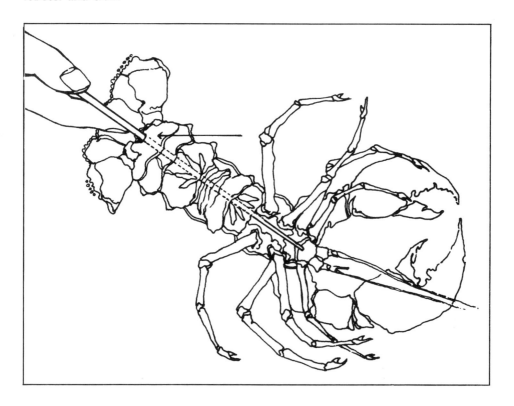

The second method used by many professional chefs who want good raw lobster is actually very quick and easy. This method is recommended for recipes in this book.

1. Turn the lobster shell-side down, insert a chopstick into the orifice at the bottom of the tail and push it all the way to the head. This will immediately desensitize the nervous system, making the lobster completely limp and relaxed.
2. Use a cleaver to cut off the claws from the body, then crack them with the back of a cleaver or nutcracker. Chop into pieces as required.
3. Lift off the head shell and discard the stomach sac (A) and gills (B) behind the head. Use a cleaver to chop the tail lengthwise into halves, then into pieces as required.

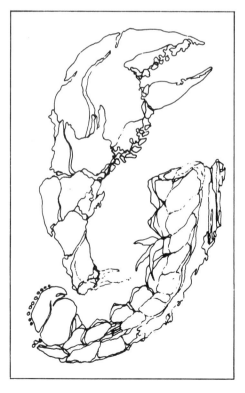
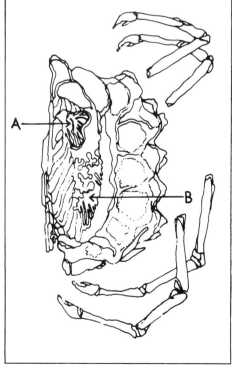

How to Shop for Shrimp and Prawns

Prawns are bigger than shrimp and have a harder shell. When shopping watch for these features:

1. The head and legs should be complete.
2. The eyes should be bright, shiny and not sunken.
3. The shell should fit tightly to the body and be firm to the touch.
4. They should have a mild sea smell.
5. The color should range from grayish green to light pink.

How to Shell Shrimp and Prawns

1. Grasp the legs on one side of the body. Peel shell by pulling the legs up over the back and then down the other side.
2. Remove the vein that runs along the back side with a toothpick or a pair of tweezers. (The vein is not harmful and is often unnoticeable in small shrimp.)

How to Prepare Squid

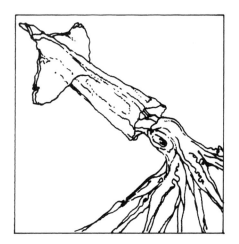 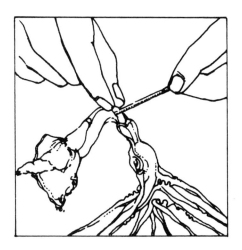

1. From the inside of the tubular body, pull out the long sword-shaped cellular backbone.

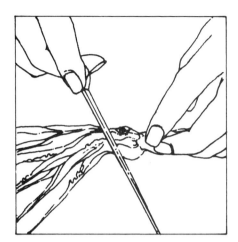

2. Separate the body from the hood by pulling them apart carefully.
3. Cut the tentacles from the head just below the eyes.

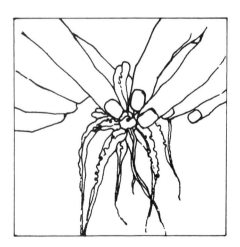
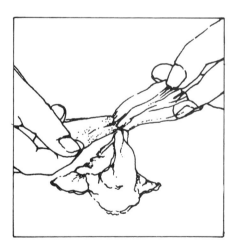

4. Find the horn-like beak between the tentacles, squeeze it out and discard it.
5. Pull off and discard the speckled membrane that covers the hood.

6. Score diagonally to form a diamond pattern.
7. Cut squid into pieces as required.

How to Prepare Fresh Oysters

Oysters should have shells closed tightly; discard them if they are loose or open. Use the following 5 steps to shuck the oysters:

1. Wearing a mitten for protection, hold an oyster with the bigger shell down on a board.
2. Using an oyster knife or beer can opener, slip the tool between the shells at the hinge.
3. Use a twisting action to pry the shells apart.
4. Sever the muscle to separate the oyster from the shell.
5. Wash and drain.

Fish

Cod and Spinach Soup

A nutritious, low-calorie way to serve jade-colored spinach soup with fish.

Substitution: haddock, Boston bluefish, red snapper

¾	lb.	Cod fillets, cut into bite-size pieces	375	g
		Oil for deep-frying		
4	cups	Soup stock (chicken or fish)	1	L
½	cup	Mushrooms, cut into quarters	125	mL
2	Tbsp.	Carrots, sliced	30	mL
½	tsp.	Salt	2	mL
	dash	Pepper		dash
3	slices	Ginger, sliced thin	3	slices
1	cup	Fresh spinach, washed and cut in half	250	mL
2	stalks	Green onion, chopped	2	stalks

1. Heat oil and deep-fry fish for 2 minutes. Remove and discard oil.
2. In the wok over high heat, bring soup stock to a boil. Add fish, mushrooms, carrots, salt to taste, pepper and ginger and boil for 5 minutes.
3. Add green onion and spinach and boil for 2 more minutes. Serve hot.

Cod Tempura

A popular dish in Japan, cod tempura is gaining popularity in North America. Great with Chili-Horseradish Sauce.

Substitution: prawns, oysters

1	lb.	Cod fillets, cut into bite-size pieces	500	g
¼	tsp.	Salt	1	mL
¼	tsp.	Lemon juice	1	mL
2	cups	Flour	500	mL
3		Egg yolks, beaten with	3	
2	cups	Ice water	500	mL
		Ice for chilling		
		Oil for deep-frying		

Chili-Horseradish Sauce

Combine the following ingredients.

1	cup	Mayonnaise	250	mL
3	Tbsp.	Horseradish	45	mL
1½	tsp.	Chili or Tabasco Sauce	7	mL

1. Wash fish, drain and dry on paper towel.
2. Sprinkle salt and lemon juice over fish.
3. Sift flour 4 times and gradually add to egg solution, mixing gently. Place bowl containing batter over ice.
4. Drop fish into the batter.
5. Heat oil. Use a fork to pick up fish and deep-fry a few pieces at a time until golden brown. Serve with Chili-Horseradish Sauce.

Smoked Cod

Substitution: mackerel, salmon

1	lb.	Cod, cut into 3 round steaks	500	g
2	Tbsp.	Soy sauce for marinating fish	30	mL
1	Tbsp.	Cooking wine for marinating fish	15	mL
		Oil for deep-frying		
¼	cup	Sugar	60	mL
2	Tbsp.	Soy sauce	30	mL
1	tsp.	Ginger, minced	5	mL
1	tsp.	Cooking wine	5	mL
3	Tbsp.	Cooking oil	45	mL

1. Marinate fish with soy sauce and wine for 1 hour.
2. Heat oil for deep-frying. . Pat fish dry and deep-fry for about 10 minutes until golden brown. Remove fish and discard oil.
3. Combine sugar, soy sauce, ginger and wine in a small bowl.
4. Heat cooking oil. Add fish and soy sauce mixture. Bring to a boil and simmer until sauce thickens. Remove fish and serve.

Braised Ling Cod in Onion Sauce

Ling cod is a lean fish whose flesh turns white when cooked. The onion sauce will eliminate the fishy smell and add great flavor to this low-calorie fish.

Substitution: black cod, pollock, whitefish, pike, pickerel

3	Tbsp.	Cooking oil	45	mL
1	lb.	Ling cod, cut into 3 steaks	500	g
1/2	cup	Flour	125	mL
1	Tbsp.	Green onion, minced	15	mL
1	Tbsp.	Ginger, minced	15	mL
1	Tbsp.	Garlic, minced	15	mL
1	Tbsp.	Cooking wine	15	mL
1/2	tsp.	Salt	2	mL
1	Tbsp.	Soy sauce	15	mL
1	tsp.	Sugar	5	mL
1	tsp.	Cornstarch, dissolved in	5	mL
1/4	cup	Water	60	mL
1	tsp.	Vinegar	5	mL

1. Heat cooking oil in wok.
2. Coat steaks with flour.
3. Add the steaks to wok and fry for 5 minutes. Turn and cook on the other side for another 5 minutes.
4. Combine green onion, ginger, garlic, cooking wine, salt, soy sauce, sugar, cornstarch mixture and vinegar. When fish is done, pour mixture into wok with fish and bring to a boil. Serve hot.

Eel with Vegetables

Substitution: squid, prawns

¾	lb.	Eel	375	g
1	Tbsp.	Salt	15	mL
1		Egg white	1	
1	tsp.	Salt	5	mL
1	Tbsp.	Cooking wine	15	mL
		Oil for deep-frying		
3	Tbsp.	Cooking oil	45	mL
½	cup	Mushrooms, cut into halves	125	mL
½	cup	Broccoli flowerets	125	mL
¼	cup	Carrot, sliced	60	mL
¼	cup	Red pepper, cut into squares	60	mL
1	slice	Ginger, shredded	1	slice
2	stalks	Green onion, chopped fine	2	stalks
1	tsp.	Garlic, minced	5	mL
	dash	Salt		dash
1	tsp.	Sugar	5	mL
1	Tbsp.	Oyster sauce	15	mL
	dash	Pepper		dash
½	tsp.	Sesame seed oil	2	mL
1	tsp.	Cornstarch, dissolved in	5	mL
3	Tbsp.	Water	45	mL

1. Bone eel and cut it into bite-size pieces. Coat with salt, then wash under running water until meat is clean. Drain and dry.
2. Marinate with egg white, salt and wine for 10 minutes.
3. Heat oil for deep-frying and deep-fry eel for 2 minutes. Remove and drain. Clean wok.
4. Heat cooking oil. Stir-fry mushrooms, broccoli, carrot, red pepper, ginger, green onion, garlic and a dash of salt for 2 minutes. Add eel, sugar, oyster sauce, pepper and sesame seed oil and mix well. Thicken with cornstarch solution. Serve hot.

Steamed Eel in Blackbean Sauce

Substitution: mackerel, cod, oysters, prawns

1½	lb.	Eel, cut into bite-size pieces	750	g
2	tsp.	Salt	10	mL
1		Red chili pepper, shredded	1	
2	tsp.	Garlic, minced	10	mL
2	slices	Ginger, shredded	2	slices
1	Tbsp.	Salted blackbeans, mashed	15	mL
1	tsp.	Soy sauce	5	mL
2	tsp.	Sugar	10	mL
	dash	Pepper		dash
1	tsp.	Sesame seed oil	5	mL
2	Tbsp.	Cooking oil	30	mL
2	stalks	Green onion, chopped	2	stalks

1. To clean eel, coat with salt, then rinse under running water. Dry with paper towels.
2. Combine chili pepper, garlic, ginger, blackbeans, soy sauce, sugar, pepper, sesame seed oil and cooking oil in a bowl.
3. Marinate eel in the mixture for 20 minutes. Transfer eel to a plate and steam in wok over high heat for 10 minutes. (See "How to Steam Seafood," p. 14.)
4. Sprinkle with green onion. Serve hot.

Fried Eel

A garlicky way to turn eel meat into a mouth-watering dish.

Substitution: squid, prawns

¾	lb.	Eel	375	g
2	tsp.	Salt	10	mL
		Oil for deep-frying		
¼	cup	Cooking oil	60	mL
	dash	Pepper		dash
½	tsp.	Sugar	2	mL
3	Tbsp.	Soy sauce	45	mL
2	tsp.	Cooking wine	10	mL
2	tsp.	Cornstarch, dissolved in	10	mL
1	Tbsp.	Water	15	mL
1	Tbsp.	Garlic, minced	15	mL
1	Tbsp.	Sesame seed oil	15	mL
	dash	Pepper		dash
2	slices	Ginger, shredded	2	slices

1. Cut the eel into sections, then cut each section lengthwise into quarters.
2. Put cut eel into a large bowl and mix with the salt, then wash under running water until all the salt has been removed. Drain and dry with paper towel.
3. Heat oil for deep-frying and deep-fry eel for 1 minute. Remove and drain. Clean wok.
4. Pour half of the cooking oil into the wok and reheat. Add eel, pepper, sugar, soy sauce and cooking wine. Stir-fry for 2 minutes. Thicken with cornstarch solution. Remove to a serving plate. Make a well in the center and place minced garlic in it.
5. Heat remaining cooking oil and sesame seed oil until smoking hot. Pour it over the garlic. Sprinkle with pepper and garnish with ginger. Serve hot.

Fried Flounder

Next to cod, flounder is one of the most important fish caught in the Atlantic. Because the flesh is relatively thin, it is perfect for fast cooking. Serve this dish with oyster sauce, plum sauce or sweet-and-sour sauce.

Substitution: sole, snapper, rock cod, perch

1½	lb.	Whole flounder	750	g
2	tsp.	Cooking wine	10	mL
1	slice	Ginger, minced	1	slice
1	tsp.	Salt	5	mL
1	Tbsp.	Cornstarch	15	mL
		Oil for deep-frying		
4	leaves	Lettuce	4	leaves

1. Scale and clean fish thoroughly. Pat dry with paper towels. If the fish is thick, score with a knife in 2 places along the backbone.
2. Marinate the fish with wine, ginger and salt for 2 minutes. Dust the fish with cornstarch.
3. Heat oil for deep-frying to medium heat. Hold the fish by the tail and slowly lower it into the hot oil. Deep-fry for about 5 minutes. Turn the heat to high and continue to deep-fry for another minute until the fish is golden brown. Remove and drain. Garnish with lettuce.

Steamed Flounder

The best way to enjoy the pure flavor of flounder is by steaming it.

Substitution: rock cod, shad, sole, perch

1½	lb.	Whole flounder	750	g
3	stalks	Green onion, halved and cut into strips	3	stalks
2	Tbsp.	Cooking oil	30	mL
1	Tbsp.	Ginger, shredded	15	mL
2	stalks	Green onion, chopped fine	2	stalks
2	Tbsp.	Soy sauce	30	mL

1. Scale and clean fish thoroughly. Pat dry with paper towels.
2. Using an oval plate, arrange onion stalks across the length of the plate.
3. Place the blind side of the flounder on top of the green onions.
4. Using high heat, steam fish in wok for 15 minutes. (See "How to Steam Seafood," p. 14.)
5. While waiting for the fish to cook, use a small pot to boil the cooking oil.
6. After steaming, discard the green onion stalks and place ginger and chopped green onion on top of the fish. Pour hot oil over the fish, then soy sauce. Serve immediately.

Chili Haddock Soup

You can adjust the spices below to suit your taste buds.

Substitution: cod, pollock, whitefish

2	Tbsp.	Cooking oil	300	mL
1/2	tsp.	Ginger, minced	2	mL
1/4	cup	Onion, chopped	60	mL
1	lb.	Haddock fillets, cut into small cubes	500	g
1/2	cup	Carrot, diced	125	mL
1/2	cup	Celery, diced	125	mL
1/2	cup	Tomato, cut into wedges	125	mL
1/2	tsp.	Salt	2	mL
1	tsp.	Soy sauce	5	mL
1/4	tsp.	Pepper	1	mL
1/2	tsp.	Chili powder	2	mL
2	cups	Soup stock (chicken or fish)	500	mL
1	Tbsp.	Green onion, chopped fine	15	mL
	drops	Sesame seed oil		drops

1. Heat cooking oil. Add ginger and onion and brown.
2. Add fish and sauté for 4 minutes, then add carrot, celery, tomato, salt, soy sauce, pepper and chili powder. Stir-fry for 1 minute.
3. Add soup stock, cover and simmer for 15 minutes. Sprinkle with green onion. Add sesame seed oil and serve hot.

Almond Haddock

Substitution: cod, pollock, whitefish, pike, pickerel

10	oz.	Haddock fillets	300	g
½	tsp.	Salt	2	mL
½	tsp.	Ginger, minced	2	mL
1	Tbsp.	Cooking wine	15	mL
	drops	Sesame seed oil		drops
	dash	Pepper		dash
½	cup	Cornstarch	125	mL
1	large	Egg, beaten	1	large
½	cup	Almond flakes	125	mL
		Oil for deep-frying		
		Lettuce, tomato and lemon for garnish		

1. Cut fillets into small fish sticks.
2. Marinate fish with salt, ginger, wine, sesame seed oil and pepper for 20 minutes.
3. Pat fish dry. Coat with cornstarch. Dip in beaten egg and then coat thoroughly with almond flakes.
4. Heat oil. Using medium heat, deep-fry fish for about 5 minutes until brown. Remove and drain oil. Garnish with lettuce leaves, tomato slices and lemon wedges.

Halibut Steaks in Ginger Sauce, page 39

Haddock and Green Beans

Substitution: scallops, crab, shrimp, whitefish

1	lb.	Haddock fillets, cut along grain into thin slices	500	g
2	Tbsp.	Soy sauce	30	mL
1	Tbsp.	Cornstarch	15	mL
2	Tbsp.	Cooking oil	30	mL
2	slices	Ginger, shredded	2	slices
2	stalks	Green onion, chopped	2	stalks
1	cup	Green beans, cut into pieces	250	mL
1/4	cup	Soup stock (chicken or fish)	60	mL
2	tsp.	Sugar	10	mL
2	tsp.	Vinegar	10	mL
1/2	tsp.	Salt	2	mL

1. Marinate fish with soy sauce and cornstarch for 15 minutes.
2. Heat half of the cooking oil. Stir-fry ginger and green onion for 1 minute. Add green beans and stir-fry for 3 minutes. Remove and set aside.
3. Heat remaining cooking oil. Add fish and stir-fry for 4 minutes. Add green beans, soup stock, sugar, vinegar and salt and cook for another 2 or 3 minutes. Serve hot.

Steamed Whole Red Snapper in Orange Sauce, page 53

Diced Haddock in Hot Blackbean Sauce

Substitution: cod, perch, flounder

1	lb.	Haddock fillets, cut into bite-size squares	500	g
½	tsp.	Salt	2	mL
2	tsp.	Cooking wine	10	mL
¼	tsp.	White pepper	1	mL
		Oil for deep-frying		
2	Tbsp.	Cooking oil	30	mL
1	tsp.	Salted blackbeans, mashed	5	mL
1	tsp.	Garlic, chopped	5	mL
1	tsp.	Ginger, chopped	5	mL
3	Tbsp.	Soup stock (chicken or fish)	45	mL
1	tsp.	Chili pepper, chopped (optional)	5	mL
2	tsp.	Green onion, chopped	10	mL
1	tsp.	Cornstarch, dissolved in	5	mL
¼	cup	Water	60	mL

1. Marinate fish with salt, wine and pepper.
2. Heat oil and deep-fry fish for 1 minute. Remove fish and drain oil.
3. Heat cooking oil until hot. Stir-fry blackbeans, garlic and ginger for 20 seconds. Add fish, soup stock, chili pepper and green onion. Cook for another 30 seconds and thicken with cornstarch solution. Serve immediately.

Haddock Steaks in Mushroom Sauce

Substitution: cod, whitefish

3		Haddock round steaks	3	
1	tsp.	Salt	5	mL
½	cup	Flour	125	mL
3	Tbsp.	Cooking oil	45	mL
4	slices	Ginger, slivered	4	slices
2	stalks	Green onion, chopped fine	2	stalks
1	tsp.	Cornstarch, dissolved in	5	mL
¾	cup	Water	175	mL
1	Tbsp.	Soy sauce	15	mL
1	tsp.	Sugar	5	mL
	dash	Pepper		dash
	drops	Sesame seed oil		drops
¼	cup	Mushrooms, sliced	60	mL

1. Sprinkle fish sparingly with salt on both sides, then coat with flour.
2. Heat the cooking oil and fry fish for 5 minutes on each side.
3. While fish is cooking, combine ginger, green onion, cornstarch solution, soy sauce, sugar, pepper, sesame seed oil and mushrooms. Stir well.
4. When fish is done, pour the sauce mixture over it. Bring to a boil and serve with steamed rice, noodles or potatoes.

Hake with Walnuts

This dish can be prepared beforehand and can be served with any Chinese dipping sauce.

Substitution: plaice, snapper, cod, sole

10	oz.	Hake fillets	300	g
2	stalks	Green onion, chopped fine	2	stalks
½	tsp.	Salt	2	mL
	dash	Pepper		dash
½	tsp.	Sugar	2	mL
1	Tbsp.	Cornstarch	15	mL
1	tsp.	Soy sauce	5	mL
1	tsp.	Cooking wine	5	mL
1		Egg	1	
½	cup	Walnuts, chopped fine	125	mL
		Oil for deep-frying		

1. Cut fish into finger-size pieces.
2. Mix green onion, salt, pepper, sugar, cornstarch, soy sauce, wine and egg. Stir well.
3. Dip the fish pieces in the mixture and then in the chopped walnuts.
4. Deep-fry for 5 minutes until golden. Remove and drain oil. Serve hot.

Halibut Steaks in Ginger Sauce

The fish can be fried ahead of time; just cook the sauce at serving time, reheat the fish and pour the sauce over it.

Substitution: cod, salmon, whitefish, pike, pickerel

3		Halibut round steaks	3	
1	tsp.	Salt	5	mL
½	cup	Flour	125	mL
3	Tbsp.	Cooking oil	45	mL
4	slices	Ginger, slivered	4	slices
2	stalks	Green onion, chopped fine	2	stalks
1	Tbsp.	Cornstarch, dissolved in	15	mL
¾	cup	Water	175	mL
1	Tbsp.	Soy sauce	15	mL
1	tsp.	Sugar	5	mL
	dash	Pepper		dash
	drops	Sesame seed oil		drops

1. Sprinkle fish sparingly with salt on both sides, then coat with flour.
2. Heat cooking oil and fry fish for 5 minutes on each side.
3. While fish is cooking, combine ginger, green onion, cornstarch solution, soy sauce, sugar, pepper and sesame seed oil in a bowl. Stir well.
4. When fish is done, add the sauce mixture and bring to a boil. Excellent with steamed rice, noodles or potatoes.

Herring in Ginger Sauce

Formerly harvested for reduction to meal and oil, herring is now a prized food fish, especially valued for its roe. This tangy recipe can be prepared indoors in the wok or outdoors in a frying pan.

Substitution: trout

2		Herring	2	
1	tsp.	Salt	5	mL
1		Egg white	1	
		Oil for deep-frying		
1	Tbsp.	Cooking oil	15	mL
1	tsp.	Ginger, slivered	5	mL
1	stalk	Green onion, chopped fine	1	stalk
1	Tbsp.	Soy sauce	15	mL
1	Tbsp.	Sugar	15	mL
	drops	Sesame seed oil		drops
½	tsp.	Cooking wine	2	mL
1	tsp.	Cornstarch, dissolved in	5	mL
¼	cup	Water	60	mL

1. Scale fish and remove the inside organs. Wash and dry.
2. Sprinkle salt over fish.
3. Dip fish in egg white, then deep-fry for 10 minutes. Remove to a plate.
4. Heat cooking oil. Sauté ginger and green onion for 1 minute.
5. Add soy sauce, sugar, sesame seed oil, wine and cornstarch solution. Bring to a boil. Pour on top of the herring and serve hot with steamed rice.

Fried Mackerel Sticks

This appetizing dish can be prepared beforehand and served with ketchup or any other sauce.

Substitution: haddock, cod, pollock

1	lb.	Mackerel fillets	500	g
	dash	Salt		dash
	dash	Pepper		dash
2		Egg whites	2	
1	tsp.	Flour	5	mL
1	tsp.	Cornstarch	5	mL
		Oil for deep-frying		

1. Cut fillets along grain into finger-size pieces.
2. Sprinkle with salt and pepper.
3. Beat egg whites. Add flour, cornstarch and dash of salt. Mix into a smooth batter.
4. Dip fish into batter, heat oil and deep-fry until it turns golden brown.

Mackerel in Hot Sauce

This is a northern Chinese recipe using chili and garlic.

Substitution: tuna, cod, shad

3		Mackerel round steaks	3	
	dash	Salt		dash
½	cup	Flour	125	mL
¼	cup	Cooking oil	60	mL
1	tsp.	Hot chili sauce or Tabasco	5	mL
1	Tbsp.	Green onion, minced	15	mL
1	Tbsp.	Ginger, minced	15	mL
1	Tbsp.	Garlic, minced	15	mL
½	tsp.	Salt	1	mL
2	tsp.	Soy sauce	10	mL
2	tsp.	Sugar	10	mL
	drops	Sesame seed oil		drops
1	tsp.	Cooking wine	5	mL
1	Tbsp.	Vinegar	15	mL
½	cup	Water	125	mL
2	tsp.	Cornstarch, dissolved in	10	mL
1	Tbsp.	Water	15	mL
1	Tbsp.	Green onion, chopped fine	15	mL

1. Sprinkle fish with salt and coat with flour.
2. Heat cooking oil. Fry each side of the fish for 5 minutes until brown. Remove fish from wok and put aside.
3. Stir-fry chili sauce, green onion, ginger and garlic for 1 minute. Add salt, soy sauce, sugar, sesame seed oil, cooking wine, vinegar and water.
4. Add fish. Cook for about 3 minutes. Thicken with cornstarch solution. Remove to serving plate and sprinkle with green onion. Serve hot.

Perch and Watercress Soup

Almost any white-fleshed fish fillet is suitable for this type of soup.

Substitution: red snapper, rock cod

10	oz.	Perch fillets	300	g
1	Tbsp.	Soy sauce	15	mL
1	tsp.	Cornstarch	5	mL
2	tsp.	Cooking oil	10	mL
	dash	Pepper		dash
1¼	cups	Watercress	300	mL.
4	cups	Water or soup stock (chicken or fish)	1	L
2	slices	Ginger, shredded	2	slices
¼	tsp.	Salt	1	mL

1. Cut fish into thin slices and marinate with soy sauce, cornstarch, cooking oil and pepper for 10 minutes.
2. Wash watercress well and cut into lengths.
3. Boil water or soup stock and ginger. Add watercress and salt to taste and boil for 5 minutes. Add fish and boil for another 2 minutes. Serve hot.

Sesame Perch

This dish makes an excellent appetizer, and can be served with drinks. It's crispy and rich in flavor.

Substitution: haddock, pollock

1	lb.	Perch fillets, cut into bite-size pieces	500	g
1	slice	Ginger, shredded	1	slice
1	stalk	Green onion, chopped	1	stalk
1	Tbsp.	Rice wine or sherry	15	mL
½	tsp.	Salt	2	mL
	dash	Pepper		dash
1	tsp.	Sugar	5	mL
¼	cup	Cornstarch	60	mL
¼	cup	Flour	60	mL
1		Egg	1	
3	Tbsp.	Water	45	mL
¼	cup	Sesame seeds	60	mL
		Oil for deep-frying		

1. Marinate fish with ginger, green onion, wine, salt, pepper and sugar for 20 minutes.
2. Make smooth batter with cornstarch, flour, egg and water.
3. Dip fish in the batter and then in sesame seeds. Deep-fry for 5 minutes until brown. Serve hot.

Buttered Pickerel

A fragrant dish, buttered pickerel is nutritious and attractive. The sauce adds a smooth flavor to the texture of the fish.

Substitution: haddock, pollock, red snapper, whitefish, pike, cod

³/₄	lb.	Pickerel fillets	375	g
1	tsp.	Salt	5	mL
¹/₂	tsp.	Pepper	2	mL
3	Tbsp.	Cornstarch	45	mL
³/₄	cup	Butter	175	mL
1	clove	Garlic, minced	1	clove
2	slices	Ginger, shredded	2	slices
¹/₂	small	Cucumber, sliced	¹/₂	small
2	small	Tomatoes, sliced	2	small
1	small	Onion, chopped	1	small
1		Red chili pepper, chopped	1	
2	slices	Pineapple, cut into small wedges	2	slices
¹/₂	cup	Soup stock (chicken or fish)	125	mL
1	tsp.	Sugar	5	mL
2	tsp.	Soy sauce	10	mL
1	tsp.	Salt	5	mL
	dash	Pepper		dash
1	tsp.	Cornstarch, dissolved in	5	mL
2	Tbsp.	Water	30	mL

1. Cut fish into thin slices. Sprinkle with salt and pepper and set aside for 10 minutes. Coat with cornstarch.
2. Heat butter and fry fish for 5 minutes on each side. Remove and keep warm on serving plate. Leave butter in wok.
3. Add garlic and ginger and stir-fry for 1 minute. Add vegetables, red chili pepper, pineapple and soup stock. Simmer for 5 minutes. Season with sugar, soy sauce, salt and pepper. Thicken with cornstarch solution.
4. Pour vegetables and pineapple on fish. Serve.

Curried Pickerel Fillets

A spicy way to prepare pickerel fillets, this dish is very popular in the Far East.

Substitution: pollock, haddock, redfish, whitefish, pike, cod

1	lb.	Pickerel fillets, cut into bite-size squares	500	g
1		Egg white	1	
1	tsp.	Cornstarch	5	mL
¼	tsp.	Salt	1	mL
¼	tsp.	Pepper	1	mL
½	cup	Cornstarch for coating fish	125	mL
		Oil for deep-frying		
2	tsp.	Cooking oil	10	mL
2	tsp.	Onion, diced	10	mL
2	tsp.	Green peas	10	mL
1	tsp.	Curry powder	5	mL
1	tsp.	Sugar	5	mL
½	tsp.	Salt	2	mL
5	tsp.	Water	25	mL

1. Marinate fish with egg white, 1 tsp. cornstarch, salt and pepper.
2. Coat each piece of fish with cornstarch. Heat oil for deep-frying. Over medium heat, deep-fry fish for 2 minutes. Remove fish and drain. Remove oil.
3. Heat cooking oil. Stir-fry onion and green peas for 2 minutes. Add curry powder, sugar, salt and water. Bring to a boil.
4. Return fish to wok, stir and serve hot with steamed rice.

Plaice in Sweet-and-Sour Sauce

This recipe was first created by an emperor's chef and is now very popular in China.

Substitution: flounder, sole, whitefish, pike, pickerel

1	lb.	Plaice fillets	500	g
2	Tbsp.	Cornstarch	30	mL
		Oil for deep-frying		
2	Tbsp.	Sugar	30	mL
1	Tbsp.	Soy sauce	15	mL
1	Tbsp.	Vinegar	15	mL
1	Tbsp.	Cooking wine	15	mL
1	Tbsp.	Cornstarch	15	mL
1	Tbsp.	Cooking oil	15	mL
1	slice	Ginger, minced	1	slice
1	stalk	Green onion, chopped	1	stalk

1. Cut fish into slices and coat with cornstarch.
2. Heat oil and deep-fry fish for 5 minutes until brown. Remove and drain. In a bowl mix the sugar, soy sauce, vinegar, wine and cornstarch.
3. Heat cooking oil and stir-fry ginger and green onion. Pour in sauce mixture and stir until it thickens.
4. Add the fish and coat well. Serve hot with steamed rice.

Pollock with Lemon Sauce

Related to cod and haddock, the pollock is perhaps best known commercially as Boston bluefish. With somewhat darker flesh than cod, it nevertheless can be prepared in the same ways.

Substitution: flounder, char, sole, cod, whitefish

1	lb.	Pollock fillets, cut crosswise into medium-size squares	500	g
1		Egg white, beaten with dash of salt	1	
½	cup	Cornstarch	125	mL
		Oil for deep-frying		
3	Tbsp.	Cooking oil	45	mL
½	cup	Onion, shredded	125	mL
¼	tsp.	Lemon extract	1	mL
3	Tbsp.	Sugar	45	mL
	drops	Yellow food coloring		drops
2	Tbsp.	Vinegar	30	mL
6	slices	Fresh lemon	6	slices
1	tsp.	Cornstarch, dissolved in	5	mL
¼	cup	Water	60	mL
2	stalks	Green onion, chopped fine	2	stalks

1. Marinate fish with egg white for 30 minutes.
2. Coat each piece of fish in cornstarch. Heat oil and deep-fry fish until golden brown. Remove fish, drain oil and clean wok.
3. Heat cooking oil. Sauté onion for 20 seconds. Add mixture of lemon extract, sugar, food coloring, vinegar, lemon slices and cornstarch solution. Stir-fry and bring to a boil.
4. Return fish to wok and stir-fry for 1 minute. Garnish with green onion and serve hot.

Red Snapper Fillet Roll with Broccoli

Substitution: flounder, haddock, perch, whitefish

1	lb.	Red snapper fillets	500	g
1/4	tsp.	Salt	1	mL
1	tsp.	Cornstarch	5	mL
1/2	tsp.	Water	2	mL
1/4	cup	Ham, shredded	60	mL
3/4	cup	Broccoli stalks, cut into bite-		
		size pieces	175	mL
1/2	cup	Water	125	mL
	dash	Salt		dash
		Oil for deep-frying		
1	Tbsp.	Cooking oil	15	mL
1	tsp.	Garlic, minced	5	mL
2	Tbsp.	Carrot, sliced thin	30	mL
1/4	tsp.	Salt	1	mL
1/4	tsp.	Pepper	1	mL
1/4	tsp.	Sesame seed oil	1	mL
1/2	tsp.	Cornstarch, dissolved in	2	mL
1/4	cup	Water	60	mL

1. Cut each fish fillet in half horizontally. Marinate the thin slices in salt, cornstarch and water.
2. Sprinkle a little cornstarch on a plate. Place a piece of sliced fillet on plate. Add shredded ham and roll up lengthwise. Repeat.
3. Cook broccoli in boiling water with salt and a little oil for 3 minutes. Remove and put under cold running water for 2 minutes. Dry with paper towel.
4. Deep-fry fish rolls for 3 minutes. Remove from oil and drain.
5. Stir-fry garlic in cooking oil. Add carrot, broccoli stalks and the fish rolls.
6. Combine salt, pepper, sesame seed oil and cornstarch solution. Pour in wok and stir until mixture thickens. Serve hot.

Red Snapper and Broccoli Stir-Fry

This is a quick and colorful way to prepare fish fillets.

Substitution: salmon, cod, halibut, whitefish

1	lb.	Red snapper fillets, sliced	500	g
1		Egg white, beaten with dash of salt	1	
1	tsp.	Cooking wine	5	mL
	dash	Salt		dash
1	cup	Broccoli, sliced diagonally	250	mL
1	small	Carrot, sliced diagonally	1	small
3	Tbsp.	Water	45	mL
2	Tbsp.	Cooking oil	30	mL
3	slices	Ginger	3	slices
1	small	Onion	1	small
1	Tbsp.	Soy sauce	15	mL
1	Tbsp.	Cornstarch, dissolved in	15	mL
1/4	cup	Water	60	mL
1/4	tsp.	Sugar	1	mL
	drops	Sesame seed oil		drops

1. Marinate fish with egg white, wine and dash of salt for 30 minutes.
2. Heat wok and add broccoli, carrot and water. Cover with a lid and cook over high heat for 3 minutes. Remove to a plate when done. Discard water.
3. Heat cooking oil, then add ginger and onion and brown for 1 minute.
4. Fry fish for 2 minutes. Add soy sauce, cornstarch solution, sugar and sesame seed oil. Stir until thoroughly cooked. Add steamed vegetables, mix and serve immediately.

Red Snapper with Vegetables

A quick and easy last-minute supper dish.

Substitution: haddock, Boston bluefish, cod, turbot, whitefish

1½	lb.	Red snapper fillets, cut into thick strips	750	g
½	cup	Cooking oil	125	mL
1	cup	Onions, sliced thin	250	mL
1	cup	Carrots, sliced thin	250	mL
2	cups	Broccoli flowerets	500	mL
1	cup	Green pepper, cut into strips	250	mL
1	cup	Mushrooms, sliced	250	mL
2	Tbsp.	Oyster sauce	30	mL
2	cups	Tomato, cut into wedges	500	mL
	dash	Salt		dash
	dash	Pepper		dash
2	Tbsp.	Cornstarch, dissolved in	30	mL
2	Tbsp.	Water	30	mL

1. Stir-fry fish in half the cooking oil, stirring gently for 5 minutes.
2. Add remaining cooking oil and stir-fry onions, carrots, broccoli, green pepper and mushrooms 3 to 5 minutes or until vegetables are tender crisp. Add oyster sauce and mix well. Add fish, tomato, salt and pepper and stir gently.
3. Thicken with cornstarch solution. Serve hot.

Red Snapper with Pineapple

Substitution: haddock, Boston bluefish, cod, turbot, whitefish

1	lb.	Red snapper fillets, cut into small cubes	500	g
1	Tbsp.	Cornstarch	15	mL
1½	Tbsp.	Soy sauce	25	mL
	dash	Pepper		dash
3	Tbsp.	Cooking oil	45	mL
1	tsp.	Ginger, minced	5	mL
1	clove	Garlic, minced	1	clove
1		Carrot, sliced diagonally	1	
1	medium	Red pepper, cut into small squares	1	medium
1	medium	Green pepper, cut into small squares	1	medium
1	cup	Pineapple chunks or cubes, drained	250	mL

1. Marinate fish with cornstarch, soy sauce and pepper.
2. Heat wok, add cooking oil and brown ginger and garlic for 1 minute.
3. Add fish and stir-fry for 4 minutes.
4. Add remaining ingredients and stir-fry for another 2 minutes. Serve immediately.

Steamed Red Snapper in Orange Sauce

This recipe is ideal for any medium-firm white-fleshed fish. A nutritious and light dish, it is delicious and easily digested.

Substitution: perch, cod, whitefish, pike, pickerel

1		Whole red snapper	1	
1	tsp.	Salt	5	mL
½	tsp.	Pepper	2	mL
3	Tbsp.	Cornstarch	45	mL
2	Tbsp.	Cooking oil	30	mL
1	medium	Onion, chopped fine	1	medium
2	tsp.	Garlic, minced	10	mL
2	slices	Ginger, shredded	2	slices
½	tsp.	Orange rind	2	mL
1	Tbsp.	Orange juice concentrate	15	mL
1	Tbsp.	Soy sauce	15	mL
	dash	Pepper		dash
2	stalks	Green onion, chopped fine	2	stalks
6		Orange slices	6	

1. Coat fish with salt, pepper and cornstarch and set aside for 10 minutes.
2. Steam fish in the wok over high heat for 10 minutes per pound. (See "How to Steam Seafood," p. 14.) Remove to serving dish and keep warm. Discard water.
3. To prepare the sauce, heat cooking oil in wok. Stir-fry onion, garlic and ginger for 1 minute. Add orange rind, orange juice concentrate, soy sauce and pepper. Bring to a boil and simmer 2 minutes.
4. Pour sauce over fish, sprinkle with green onion and garnish with orange slices.

Salmon and Corn Soup

Substitution: cod, char, whitefish, pike, pickerel

6	cups	Soup stock (chicken or fish)	1.5	L
	drops	Sesame oil		drops
1	tsp.	Soy sauce	5	mL
¼	tsp.	Salt	1	mL
¼	cup	Salmon fillet, chopped fine	60	mL
1	can	Sweet corn	1	can
2		Egg whites, beaten with dash of salt	2	
2	Tbsp.	Cornstarch, dissolved in	30	mL
¼	cup	Water	60	mL
	dash	Pepper		dash
1	stalk	Green onion, chopped fine	1	stalk

1. Boil the soup stock, sesame oil, soy sauce and salt for 5 minutes.
2. Add fish and sweet corn and boil for 3 minutes.
3. While soup is boiling hot, pour the egg white slowly and gently into the soup so that threads are formed.
4. Add cornstarch solution to the soup, stir well and sprinkle with pepper and green onion before serving.

Salmon Steaks in Hot Sauce

A special spicy way to enjoy the flaky texture and delicious taste of salmon steaks. This dish can be cooked indoors or out.

Substitution: halibut, char, whitefish, pike, pickerel

1	lb.	Salmon, cut into 3 round steaks	500	g
½	tsp.	Salt	2	mL
½	cup	Flour	125	mL
3	Tbsp.	Cooking oil	45	mL
1	Tbsp.	Chili sauce	15	mL
1	Tbsp.	Green onion, chopped	15	mL
1	Tbsp.	Ginger, minced	15	mL
1	Tbsp.	Garlic, minced	15	mL
1	Tbsp.	Cooking wine	15	mL
1	Tbsp.	Soy sauce	15	mL
1	tsp.	Sugar	5	mL
½	tsp.	Vinegar	2	mL
1	tsp.	Cornstarch, dissolved in	5	mL
¼	cup	Water	60	mL

1. Coat fish with salt and flour.
2. Heat cooking oil.
3. Put fish in wok and fry for 5 minutes, then turn and cook the other side for another 5 minutes.
4. Add remaining ingredients, bring to a boil and serve with rice or potatoes.

Salmon Steaks in Creamed Corn

Substitution: halibut, char, whitefish, pike, pickerel

1	lb.	Salmon, cut into 3 round steaks	500	g
½	tsp.	Salt	2	mL
½	cup	Flour	125	mL
3	Tbsp.	Cooking oil	45	mL
¼	cup	Creamed corn	60	mL
1	Tbsp.	Green onion, chopped	15	mL
1	Tbsp.	Ginger, minced	15	mL
1	Tbsp.	Garlic, minced	15	mL
1	Tbsp.	Cooking wine	15	mL
1	Tbsp.	Soy sauce	15	mL
1	tsp.	Cornstarch, dissolved in	5	mL
¼	cup	Water	60	mL

1. Coat fish with salt and flour.
2. Heat cooking oil.
3. Put fish in wok and fry for 5 minutes, then turn and cook the other side for another 5 minutes.
4. Add remaining ingredients, bring to a boil and serve hot.

Steamed Salmon

Steaming is one of the simplest ways and probably the best way to cook fish – especially when it comes to salmon.

Substitution: trout, char, mackerel, whitefish, pike, pickerel

1½	lb.	Salmon, cut into 4 round steaks	750	g
	dash	Salt		dash
	dash	Pepper		dash
4	slices	Lemon or lime	4	slices
2	Tbsp.	Cooking oil	30	mL
2	Tbsp.	Green onion, chopped	30	mL
2	slices	Ginger, shredded	2	slices
1	Tbsp.	Soy sauce	15	mL
4	sprigs	Parsley	4	sprigs

1. Sprinkle fish with salt and pepper. Top each steak with lemon slice. Arrange on plate and steam fish for 10 to 15 minutes. (See "How to Steam Seafood," p. 14.) Remove and put aside.
2. Meanwhile, heat cooking oil. Stir-fry ginger and green onion for 1 minute. Add soy sauce and mix well. Spoon mixture onto each fish steak. Garnish with parsley. Serve hot.

Seabass Toast

A clever way to use seabass fillets to make an appetizer. When cooking is done, seabass toast can be refrigerated and deep-fried at serving time. A popular attraction.

Substitution: walleye fillets

10	oz.	Seabass fillets, skinned and minced	300	g
2	strips	Bacon, chopped fine	2	strips
1	stalk	Green onion, chopped fine	1	stalk
	dash	Pepper		dash
	drops	Sesame seed oil		drops
½	cup	Onion, chopped fine	125	mL
¼	tsp.	Ginger, minced	2	mL
1	tsp.	Salt	5	mL
3	Tbsp.	Flour	45	mL
1	tsp.	Cornstarch	5	mL
¼	cup	Water	60	mL
8	slices	White sandwich bread, crust removed	8	slices
		Oil for deep-frying		

1. Mix minced fish, bacon, green onion, pepper, sesame seed oil, onion, ginger, salt, flour, cornstarch and water in a bowl.
2. Cut slices of bread in half and spread fish mixture over each piece.
3. Deep-fry for 2 minutes until golden brown. Serve with H.P. Sauce or any sauce of your choice.

Smelt Kabobs

Smelts are delicate, small fish. The flesh has a sweet flavor and the bones are fine and edible, particularly when deep-fried.

Substitution: scallop, prawns

1	lb.	Smelt, washed and dried, heads removed	500	g
½	tsp.	Salt	2	mL
1	Tbsp.	Soy sauce	15	mL
1	Tbsp.	Cooking wine	15	mL
	dash	Pepper		dash
1	medium	Green pepper, cut into small squares	1	medium
1	medium	Red pepper, cut into small squares	1	medium
16		Mushrooms, whole	16	
16		Cherry tomatoes	16	
8	small	Bamboo skewers	8	small
		Oil for deep-frying		

1. Marinate fish with salt, soy sauce, wine and pepper for 15 minutes.
2. On the skewers, alternate smelt and vegetables.
3. Deep-fry for 10 minutes and serve over hot rice or noodles.

Deep Fried Smelt

Smelt is often cooked and served whole. This dish can be served with any sauce of your choice.

Substitution: sole

1	lb.	Whole smelt	500	g
½	tsp.	Salt	2	mL
1	Tbsp.	Soy sauce	15	mL
1	Tbsp.	Cooking wine	15	mL
	dash	Pepper		dash
1		Egg, beaten	1	
½	cup	Cornstarch	125	mL
		Oil for deep-frying		
		Tomato and lemon slices for garnish		

1. Marinate fish with salt, soy sauce, wine and pepper for 15 minutes.
2. Pat fish dry. Dip it in beaten egg and then coat it completely with cornstarch.
3. Heat oil in wok. Deep-fry fish using medium heat for 10 minutes until golden brown.
4. Remove fish, drain oil and arrange on serving plate. Garnish with tomatoes and lemon slices. Serve hot or cold.

Crispy-Skinned Sole

Substitution: flounder, plaice

2	cups	Chicken stock	500	mL
3	Tbsp.	Lemon juice	45	mL
1	Tbsp.	Lemon rind, chopped	15	mL
1	tsp.	Ginger, minced	5	mL
1	Tbsp.	Green onion, chopped	15	mL
2	Tbsp.	Sugar	30	mL
1	Tbsp.	Cornstarch, dissolved in	15	mL
1/4	cup	Water	60	mL
1 1/2	lb.	Whole sole	750	g
1	cup	Flour	250	mL
	dash	Salt		dash
	dash	Pepper		dash
1	Tbsp.	Oil	15	mL
1	cup	Water	250	mL
2		Egg whites	2	
2	Tbsp.	Cornstarch	30	mL
		Oil for deep-frying		
5	stalks	Green onion, chopped	5	stalks
1		Lemon, sliced	1	

1. Prepare lemon sauce by boiling chicken stock, lemon juice and rind, ginger, green onion and sugar in wok. Simmer for 5 minutes. Thicken with cornstarch solution. Set aside. Keep warm.
2. Clean fish.
3. Prepare a smooth batter with flour, salt, pepper, oil, water and egg whites.
4. Sprinkle fish thoroughly with cornstarch. Dip fish into batter to coat completely. Deep-fry fish for 10 minutes until golden brown.
5. Remove fish, drain oil and put fish on serving plate. Garnish with lemon and green onion. Pour lemon sauce over fish. Serve hot.

Sole with Tomato Sauce

This dish is highly recommended for entertaining. The sole can be deep-fried ahead of time; just make the sauce, vegetables and rice at serving time.

Substitution: flounder, chad

1	lb.	Sole fillets, cut crosswise into medium-size squares	500	g
1		Egg white, beaten with dash of salt	1	
½	cup	Cornstarch	125	mL
		Oil for deep-frying		
3	Tbsp.	Cooking oil	45	mL
½	cup	Onion, shredded	125	mL
3	Tbsp.	Sugar	45	mL
2	Tbsp.	Vinegar	30	mL
¼	cup	Ketchup	60	mL
1	Tbsp.	Cooking wine	15	mL
	drops	Sesame seed oil		drops
1	Tbsp.	Cornstarch	15	mL
¼	cup	Water	60	mL
¼	cup	Green peas	60	mL
2	stalks	Green onion, chopped fine	2	stalks

1. Marinate fish with egg white for 30 minutes.
2. Coat each piece of fish in cornstarch. Heat oil for deep-frying and deep-fry fish for 5 minutes until golden brown. Remove fish and discard oil.
3. Heat wok, add cooking oil and wait until smoke begins to rise. Stir-fry onion for a minute and add a mixture of sugar, vinegar, ketchup, wine, sesame seed oil, cornstarch, water and green peas. Bring to a boil.
4. Return fish and stir. Garnish with green onion. Serve with steamed rice.

Steamed Sole with Cream Sauce

Substitution: haddock, cod, sole, flounder

1	lb.	Sole fillets	500	g
1	tsp.	Salt	5	mL
1	tsp.	Cooking wine	5	mL
3	stalks	Green onion, halved and cut into strips	3	stalks
1	Tbsp.	Ginger, minced	15	mL
1	Tbsp.	Cooking oil	15	mL
3	slices	Ginger	3	slices
1/2	cup	Soup stock (chicken or fish)	125	mL
1	Tbsp.	Mushrooms, sliced	15	mL
2	tsp.	Ham, diced	10	mL
2	tsp.	Green peas	10	mL
1/2	tsp.	Salt	2	mL
1/4	tsp.	Pepper	1	mL
1/2	tsp.	Cornstarch	2	mL
2	Tbsp.	Water	30	mL
2	tsp.	Milk	10	mL
2	stalks	Green onion, chopped fine	2	stalks

1. Wash the fish fillets and dry them thoroughly.
2. Marinate fish with salt, wine, green onion strips and minced ginger for 5 minutes. Place on oval plate.
3. Steam fish over high heat for 15 minutes. (See "How to Steam Seafood," p. 14.)
4. Heat cooking oil in the wok. Stir-fry the ginger slices for 30 seconds. Add soup stock, mushrooms, ham, green peas, salt and pepper. Bring to a boil. Thicken with cornstarch, water and milk. Pour the sauce over the fish and serve, garnished with chopped green onion.

Steamed Trout

Another easy way to steam fish. The original flavor is enhanced with ginger and onion in this low-calorie dish.

Substitution: perch, pickerel, seabass

1⅓	lb.	Whole trout	600	g
1	tsp.	Salt	5	mL
2	stalks	Green onion, slivered	2	stalks
2	Tbsp.	Ginger, shredded	30	mL
3	Tbsp.	Cooking oil	45	mL
2	Tbsp.	Soy sauce	30	mL

1. Remove the head and gills, scale and gut the fish. Wash and drain.
2. Score the inside of the fish with 3 cuts in the thickest section. This allows even cooking of the fish.
3. Sprinkle fish with salt and arrange skin side up on an oval plate.
4. Place in wok, cover and steam for 10 minutes over high heat. (See "How to Steam Seafood," p. 14.)
5. Remove fish from wok and sprinkle green onion and ginger over it.
6. Heat cooking oil until smoking and pour it over fish. Add soy sauce and serve.

Rainbow Trout in Ginger Sauce

This dish can be prepared indoors in the wok or outdoors in a frying pan.

Substitution: smelt, pike

1⅓	lb.	Whole rainbow trout	600	g
1	tsp.	Salt	5	mL
1		Egg white	1	
		Oil for deep-frying		
1	Tbsp.	Cooking oil	15	mL
1	tsp.	Ginger, slivered	5	mL
1	stalk	Green onion, chopped fine	1	stalk
1	Tbsp.	Soy sauce	15	mL
1	Tbsp.	Sugar	15	mL
	drops	Sesame seed oil		drops
½	tsp.	Cooking wine	2	mL
1	tsp.	Cornstarch, dissolved in	5	mL
¼	cup	Water	60	mL

1. Scale fish and remove the inside organs. Wash and dry.
2. Sprinkle salt over fish.
3. Dip fish in egg white. Heat oil for deep-frying and deep-fry fish for 10 minutes. When done, remove to a plate.
4. Heat wok and add cooking oil. Add ginger and green onion, and sauté for 1 minute.
5. Add soy sauce, sugar, sesame seed oil, wine and cornstarch solution. Bring to a boil. Pour over trout and serve hot with steamed rice.

Braised Tuna

For this dish use round tuna steaks or small whole tuna. If you use a whole fish you should score both sides with 2 or 3 diagonal cuts. This will make it cook more evenly.

Substitution: mackerel, salmon

3		Tuna round steaks	3	
1	tsp.	Salt	5	mL
½	cup	Flour	125	mL
3	Tbsp.	Cooking oil	45	mL
4	slices	Ginger, slivered	4	slices
2	stalks	Green onion, chopped fine	2	stalks
½	small	Green pepper, chopped	½	small
1	small	Tomato, cut into wedges	1	small
1	tsp.	Cornstarch	5	mL
1	tsp.	Cooking wine	5	mL
1	Tbsp.	Soy sauce	15	mL
1	tsp.	Sugar	5	mL
	dash	Pepper		dash
	drops	Sesame seed oil		drops
¾	cup	Water	175	mL

1. Sprinkle fish sparingly with salt on both sides, then coat with flour.
2. Heat cooking oil. Fry fish for 5 minutes on each side.
3. In a bowl, combine ginger, green onion, green pepper, tomato, cornstarch, wine, soy sauce, sugar, pepper, sesame seed oil and water. Stir well.
4. When fish is done, pour in sauce mixture. Bring to a boil and serve hot.

Salmon Steaks in Hot Sauce, page 55

Seafood Chow Mein

You can use an assortment of seafood for this recipe, or choose whatever is available.

2	qt.	Water	2	L
¾	lb.	Egg noodles	375	g
¼	cup	Cooking oil	60	mL
2	Tbsp.	Cooking oil	30	mL
½	tsp.	Garlic, minced	2	mL
½	tsp.	Ginger, shredded	2	mL
¾	lb.	Assortment of fish, scallops, prawns and squid	375	g
¼	cup	Snow peas, strings removed	60	mL
¼	cup	Carrot, sliced	60	mL
¼	cup	Mushrooms, cut into halves	60	mL
¼	tsp.	Salt	1	mL
	dash	Pepper		dash
½	tsp.	Cooking wine	2	mL
¼	tsp.	Sugar	1	mL
1	Tbsp.	Soy sauce	15	mL
2	tsp.	Cornstarch, dissolved in	30	mL
½	cup	Soup stock (chicken or fish)	125	mL
	drops	Sesame seed oil		drops

1. Stir egg noodles in boiling water and cook for about 3 minutes until noodles are soft and can be separated. Remove noodles to a sieve, run under cold water and drain.
2. Heat wok, add ¼ cup cooking oil and rotate wok to coat sides.
3. Spread noodles in wok, using medium heat to cook until noodles are light brown. This can be done ahead of time and noodles can be kept warm in oven.
4. Heat 2 Tbsp. cooking oil. Add garlic and ginger, then seafood, and stir-fry for 2 minutes.
5. Add all the vegetables, salt, pepper, wine and sugar, then stir-fry for 2 more minutes.
6. Add soy sauce, cornstarch solution, soup stock and sesame seed oil and bring to a boil.
7. Arrange cooked noodles on a large platter, then pour seafood mixture on top. Serve hot.

Seafood Nest, page 68-69

Seafood in a Nest

A delightful assortment of delicate sea treasures served in a specially made potato basket.

1	large	Potato	1	large
1	tsp.	Cornstarch	5	mL
		Oil for deep-frying		
¼	lb.	Scallops, cut into halves	125	g
6		Prawns, deveined	6	
6		Fish fillets, thinly sliced	6	
1		Egg white	1	
½	tsp.	Salt	2	mL
	drops	Sesame seed oil		drops
¼	cup	Cooking oil	60	mL
3	stalks	Green onion, cut into short lengths	3	stalks
½	tsp.	Ginger, minced	2	mL
½	tsp.	Garlic, minced	2	mL
4		Broccoli flowerets	4	
¼	cup	Mushrooms	60	mL
½	tsp.	Sugar	2	mL
1	Tbsp.	Cooking wine	15	mL
1	Tbsp.	Cornstarch, dissolved in	15	mL
¼	cup	Water	60	mL

1. Cut potato into thin slivers. Soak in water for 2 hours to remove excess starch. Drain well and dry in towel for 30 minutes. Place in bowl and sprinkle with cornstarch.
2. Dip 2 wire ladles in oil. Spread potato slivers evenly to cover the inside of one wire ladle. Place second wire ladle on potatoes and press 2 ladles together firmly.
3. Deep-fry until golden brown. Remove potato basket carefully from wire ladle, drain and place on platter for later use.
4. Marinate all seafood with salt, egg white and sesame seed oil for 5 minutes.

5. Heat half of cooking oil in wok and brown green onion, ginger and garlic. Add seafood and sauté until it changes color. Remove and set aside.
6. Add remaining cooking oil and stir-fry vegetables; return seafood to wok.
7. Combine sugar, wine and cornstarch solution, then add to wok and bring to a boil.
8. Transfer to potato basket and serve hot.

Seafood Soup

Varieties of seafood used in this recipe can be modified as desired.

½	lb.	Clams in the shell	250	g
		Oil for deep-frying		
¼	lb.	Red snapper or cod fillets	125	g
3	oz.	Scallops	100	g
3	cups	Soup stock (chicken or fish)	750	mL
3	oz.	Crab meat	100	g
½	tsp.	Ginger, slivered	2	mL
¼	cup	Zucchini, diced	60	mL
¼	cup	Carrot, diced	60	mL
¼	cup	Celery, diced	60	mL
2	Tbsp.	Soy sauce	30	mL
1	Tbsp.	Cooking wine	15	mL
	dash	Pepper		dash
½	tsp.	Salt	2	mL
2	stalks	Green onion, chopped fine	2	stalks

1. In a wok, boil enough water to cover clams and cook until shells open. Remove clams, discard hot water and clean wok.
2. Heat oil and deep-fry fish fillets and scallops for 2 minutes. Remove and discard oil.
3. Bring soup stock to a boil and add all seafood, ginger, wine and vegetables. Boil for 10 minutes.
4. Add salt and pepper to taste. Sprinkle green onion on top. Serve hot.

Crustaceans

Crab Fried Rice

An excellent way to serve popular fried rice.

Substitution: lobster meat, fish

6	oz.	Shrimp, shelled and deveined	175	g
½	tsp.	Cooking wine	2	mL
½	tsp.	Salt	2	mL
5	Tbsp.	Cooking oil	75	mL
3	cups	Cooked rice, cold	750	mL
2	large	Eggs, beaten with dash of salt	2	large
2	stalks	Green onion, chopped fine	2	stalks
¼	cup	Green peas, cooked	60	mL
3	slices	Ginger, shredded	3	slices
6	oz.	Crab meat	175	g
½	cup	Soup stock (chicken or fish)	125	mL
¼	cup	Milk	60	mL
2	Tbsp.	Soy sauce	30	mL
2	tsp.	Cornstarch, dissolved in	10	mL
2	Tbsp.	Water	30	mL
	dash	Pepper		dash

1. Marinate shrimp with wine and salt for 5 minutes.
2. Add half of cooking oil to wok and stir-fry shrimp until cooked.
3. Add rice and stir constantly until the rice is hot. Gently pour egg over the rice. Stir for another 2 minutes. Add green onion and green peas. Stir-fry and remove to a plate. Keep warm.
4. Heat remaining cooking oil in wok. Stir-fry ginger and crab meat. Add soup stock, milk and soy sauce and thicken with cornstarch solution. Sprinkle with pepper.
5. Pour over rice and serve hot.

Crab Meat Puffs

Ideal as an hors d'oeuvre or as a light entrée.

Substitution: shrimp

½	lb.	Crab meat, chopped fine	250	g
6	oz.	Cream cheese, softened	175	g
	dash	Garlic powder		dash
	dash	Pepper		dash
½	tsp.	Salt	2	mL
	drops	Sesame seed oil		drops
2	tsp.	Cooking wine	10	mL
1		Egg, beaten	1	
1	Tbsp.	Green onion, chopped	15	mL
60		Wonton wrappers	60	
1	Tbsp.	Cornstarch, dissolved in	15	mL
1	Tbsp.	Water to make a paste	15	mL
		Oil for deep-frying		

1. Combine crab meat, cream cheese, garlic, pepper, salt, sesame seed oil, wine, egg and green onion. Mix thoroughly.
2. Put a wonton wrapper on a plate and place a small amount of crab meat mixture in the center of the skin. Smear edges with cornstarch paste.
3. Place another wrapper on top, press edges to seal. Set aside and repeat procedure until all of mixture and wrappers are used.
4. Deep-fry. Serve with a sauce for dipping, such as sweet-and-sour sauce or plum sauce.

Crab Rangoon

This recipe uses crab meat as a filling for wontons and yields about 90 wontons. It is excellent as an appetizer or as a party snack. Frozen or canned crab meat can be used. This dish is from Rangoon, where crab is plentiful. When served with plum sauce or sweet-and-sour sauce, this appetizer can ruin your appetite for your main course. Wontons can be frozen for future use.

Substitution: shrimp, lobster meat

½	lb.	Crab meat, chopped fine	250	g
¼	tsp.	Garlic powder	1	mL
	dash	Pepper		dash
½	tsp.	Sugar	2	mL
½	tsp.	Worcestershire sauce	2	mL
¼	tsp.	Salt	1	mL
90		Wonton wrappers	90	
1		Egg yolk, beaten	1	
		Oil for deep-frying		
1	Tbsp.	Green onion, chopped fine	15	mL

1. Mix chopped crab meat with garlic, pepper, sugar, Worcestershire sauce and salt.
2. Place a wonton wrapper on a plate. Put a small amount of crab mixture in the center.
3. Fold corners of the wrapper over the top to meet in the center, moisten the edges of the square with beaten egg yolk and twist together.
4. Deep-fry until golden brown. Place on paper towel until ready to serve. Sprinkle with green onion.

Crab Meat Rolls

This dish can be prepared before your guests arrive. It makes an excellent appetizer and goes well with drinks.

Substitution: shrimp, fish

2	Tbsp.	Cooking oil	30	mL
2	cloves	Garlic, minced	2	cloves
½	lb.	Fresh pork, minced	250	g
2	Tbsp.	Mushrooms, chopped fine	30	mL
¼	cup	Carrots, shredded and cooked	60	mL
½	lb.	Crab meat, shredded	250	g
1	tsp.	Salt	5	mL
½	tsp.	Pepper	2	mL
½	tsp.	Soy sauce	2	mL
2	tsp.	Cornstarch	10	mL
24		Spring-roll wrappers	24	
1		Egg, beaten	1	
		Oil for deep-frying		

1. Heat cooking oil and stir-fry garlic. Add minced pork and stir-fry for 5 minutes until cooked. Add mushrooms and carrots and crab meat. Season with salt, pepper and soy sauce. Stir-fry for another 3 minutes. Sprinkle with cornstarch and stir well. Remove from heat and cool.
2. Put a large spoonful of crab mixture onto each wrapper and make a roll up. Tuck the ends in and roll wrap securely. Use beaten egg to seal edges.
3. Heat oil and deep-fry. Remove rolls from oil as soon as they have turned a light brown. Drain. Serve with sauce for dipping, such as sweet-and-sour sauce or plum sauce.

Crab Meat Balls

Ideal for parties and easy to prepare.

Substitution: prawns

¾	lb.	Crab meat	375	g
¼	cup	Pork fat	60	mL
½	cup	Waterchestnuts	125	mL
1	stalk	Green onion	1	stalk
2		Eggs	2	
2	Tbsp.	Cooking wine	30	mL
1	tsp.	Salt	5	mL
2	Tbsp.	Cornstarch	30	mL
1	slice	Ginger, minced	1	slice
		Oil for deep-frying		
		Cucumber, tomato slices and		
		lemon wedges for garnish		

1. Finely chop the crab meat, pork fat, waterchestnuts and green onion. Place in a bowl and mix with eggs, wine, salt, cornstarch and ginger. Blend well, then shape into small balls.
2. Heat oil over high heat, then reduce to medium heat and deep-fry crab balls for 5 minutes until golden brown. Remove and drain.
3. Garnish with cucumber, tomato and lemon. Serve hot or cold.

Stuffed Crab Claws

Another easy dish that can be prepared beforehand. Great for cocktail parties.

1	lb.	Shrimp, shelled and deveined	500	g
1	tsp.	Ginger, minced	5	mL
1	tsp.	Green onion, chopped fine	5	mL
6	Tbsp.	Pork fat, blanched and minced	90	mL
1		Egg white	1	
1	tsp.	Salt	5	mL
1	tsp.	Sugar	5	mL
	dash	Pepper		dash
2	Tbsp.	Cornstarch	30	mL
3	Tbsp.	Water	45	mL
8		Crab claws	8	
		Cornstarch for dusting		
		Oil for deep-frying		

1. Mash shrimp with the blade of a cleaver.
2. Mix all ingredients, except the crab claws. Stir thoroughly until a thick paste is formed.
3. Crack the claws and remove all of the shell except for the pointed end. Leave the meat protruding from this; it can be used as a handle.
4. Using damp fingers, coat meaty part of crab claw with a thick layer of shrimp paste. Dust with cornstarch.
5. Deep-fry crab claws for 15 minutes. Remove and drain. Serve with Worcestershire sauce.

Deep-Fried Crab

Ideal with wine at parties. Can be served with H.P. Sauce, Worcestershire sauce or any dip you prefer.

Substitution: lobster

1¾	lb.	Live crab	875	g
1	tsp.	Salt	5	mL
2		Eggs, beaten	2	
¼	cup	Cornstarch	60	mL
3	cups	Oil for deep-frying	750	mL
1	cup	Lettuce, shredded	250	mL
1		Lemon, sliced	1	

1. Prepare crab as in "How to Prepare Live Crab," p. 17. Divide the body into 8 to 10 sections, leaving the leg on each section. Drain and dry with paper towel. Crack legs.
2. Sprinkle salt lightly over crab. Dip in beaten egg and coat with cornstarch.
3. Deep-fry in hot oil for 5 minutes.
4. Make a bed of shredded lettuce on a serving plate. Arrange fried crab on top. Garnish with lemon. Serve hot.

Crab Meat with Asparagus

This is a low-calorie but delicious dish made with tender asparagus and refreshing crab meat.

Substitution: shrimp, scallops

dash		Salt		dash
2	Tbsp.	Cooking oil	30	mL
1	lb.	Asparagus spears, cut into halves	500	g
$\frac{1}{2}$	cup	Chicken stock	125	mL
$\frac{1}{4}$	cup	Milk	60	mL
6	oz.	Crab meat	175	g
dash		Pepper		dash
drops		Sesame seed oil		drops
$\frac{1}{4}$	tsp.	Salt	1	mL
1	Tbsp.	Cornstarch, dissolved in	15	mL
2	Tbsp.	Water	30	mL

1. To a wok filled with boiling water, add a dash of salt and cooking oil.
2. Add asparagus and boil for 3 minutes. When done, remove to a plate and drain.
3. Mix chicken stock with milk in a hot wok. Add crab meat, pepper, sesame seed oil and salt, then boil for 1 minute.
4. Add cornstarch solution to thicken the sauce and pour over the asparagus. Serve hot.

Crab Meat with Mushrooms

This is a popular Chinese dish the whole year round.

Substitution: fish

¼	cup	Cooking oil	60	mL
2	cups	Mushrooms, sliced	500	mL
2	stalks	Green onion, cut into bite-size pieces	2	stalks
1	tsp.	Ginger, minced	5	mL
½	tsp.	Garlic, minced	2	mL
¼	lb.	Crab meat	125	g
½	tsp.	Salt	2	mL
½	tsp.	Sugar	2	mL
1	tsp.	Cooking wine	5	mL
	drops	Sesame seed oil		drops
	dash	Pepper		dash
2	Tbsp.	Cornstarch, dissolved in	30	mL
¼	cup	Water	60	mL
2		Egg whites	2	

1. Heat half the cooking oil and stir-fry mushrooms for 2 minutes. Remove and arrange on a platter.
2. Heat the remaining cooking oil. Stir-fry green onion, ginger and garlic.
3. Add crab meat and sauté for a few seconds.
4. Add salt, sugar, wine, sesame seed oil, pepper and cornstarch solution. Bring to a boil.
5. Stir in egg whites and pour over mushrooms. Serve hot.

Crab Meat with Lettuce

A light, easily digested dish that goes well with steamed rice.

Substitution: shrimp, lobster

1	head	Romaine lettuce	1	head
3	Tbsp.	Cooking oil	45	mL
	dash	Salt		dash
1	cup	Mushrooms, cut into halves	250	mL
1		Carrot, sliced thin	1	
½	lb.	Crab meat	250	g
	dash	Salt		dash
1	Tbsp.	Cooking wine	15	mL
¼	cup	Soup stock (chicken or fish)	60	mL
1	Tbsp.	Cornstarch, dissolved in	15	mL
4	tsp.	Water	20	mL

1. Separate lettuce leaves, wash and dry.
2. Heat half of cooking oil. Stir-fry lettuce leaves with a dash of salt for 2 minutes. Place them on serving dish.
3. Heat the remaining cooking oil. Stir-fry mushrooms and carrot for about 1 minute. Add crab meat, salt, wine and soup stock. Thicken with cornstarch solution. Blend well, then pour over lettuce leaves and serve.

Crab Meat Omelet

This recipe allows you to enjoy the delicate flavor of crab meat for breakfast, or for dinner with other dishes.

Substitution: shrimp, clams

8	large	Eggs	8	large
½	tsp.	Salt	2	mL
	dash	Pepper		dash
¼	cup	Cooking oil	60	mL
4	stalks	Green onion, chopped fine	4	stalks
¼	cup	Mushrooms, chopped fine	60	mL
½	cup	Green peas	125	mL
½	lb.	Crab meat, chopped into small pieces	250	g
2	tsp.	Soy sauce	10	mL
2	Tbsp.	Cooking wine	30	mL

1. Beat eggs in bowl. Season with salt and pepper.
2. Heat ¾ of the cooking oil. Stir-fry green onion, mushrooms, peas, crab meat, soy sauce and wine for 2 minutes. Remove from wok, drain and add to beaten eggs. Mix well.
3. Heat the remaining cooking oil in wok. When oil is hot, pour egg mixture into wok. When firm, fold 2 sides over toward the middle with a spatula, remove from wok and serve.

Ginger Crab

For a stronger garlic flavor, triple the minced garlic.

Substitution: scallops (See Ginger Lobster and Ginger Oysters.)

1³/₄	lb.	Live crab	875	g
3	Tbsp.	Cooking oil	45	mL
6	slices	Ginger	6	slices
1	Tbsp.	Garlic, minced	15	mL
1	small	Onion, shredded	1	small
3	stalks	Green onion, cut into 3 sections	3	stalks
1	Tbsp.	Cooking wine	15	mL
2	Tbsp.	Soy sauce	30	mL
	dash	Pepper		dash
½	tsp.	Sugar	2	mL
	drops	Sesame seed oil		drops
1	Tbsp.	Cornstarch, dissolved in	15	mL
¼	cup	Water	125	mL

1. Prepare crab as in "How to Prepare Live Crab," p. 17. Divide the body into 8 to 10 sections, leaving a leg on each section. Drain for 30 minutes before cooking.
2. Heat cooking oil, add ginger, garlic and both onions, then stir-fry for 1 minute.
3. Add crab and stir-fry 1 minute, then add wine, soy sauce, pepper, sugar and sesame seed oil. Cover and cook over high heat for 5 minutes.
4. Add cornstarch solution and cook for 1 minute. Serve hot.

Stuffed Crab Shell

This is a fragrant, eye-catching dish, very popular in the Far East. It can be prepared beforehand.

1	Tbsp.	Vinegar	15	mL
	dash	Salt		dash
3½	lb.	Whole crab	1.75	kg
2	Tbsp.	Cooking oil	30	mL
3	stalks	Green onion, chopped fine	3	stalks
1	tsp.	Garlic, minced	5	mL
2	Tbsp.	Onion, diced	30	mL
½	tsp.	Salt	2	mL
2	Tbsp.	Bread crumbs	30	mL
2	Tbsp.	Cheese, grated	30	mL
1	tsp.	Butter	5	mL
2	tsp.	Soy sauce	10	mL
		Oil for deep-frying		

1. To a wok filled with boiling water, add vinegar and a dash of salt. Add crab and boil for 6 minutes. Remove crab from water and cool.
2. Remove shells carefully and wash them. Remove meat from crabs.
3. Heat cooking oil and stir-fry green onion, garlic, diced onion, crab meat and salt for 2 minutes. Add half of bread crumbs. Add cheese, butter and soy sauce.
4. Pack the stuffing into shells and dust with remaining bread crumbs.
5. Place stuffed crab, shell side down, in hot oil for deep-frying. Deep-fry over medium to high heat for 10 minutes. Remove and drain oil before serving.

Crab Foo Young

A fast and efficient way to serve crab meat.

Substitution: shrimp, oysters

3	Tbsp.	Cooking oil	45	mL
1	tsp.	Garlic, minced	5	mL
½	lb.	Crab meat, cooked	250	g
1	cup	Bean sprouts	250	mL
2	Tbsp.	Green onion, chopped	30	mL
¼	cup	Carrot, slivered	60	mL
¼	cup	Onion, chopped fine	60	mL
	dash	Pepper		dash
½	tsp.	Salt	2	mL
5	large	Eggs, beaten with dash of salt	5	large

1. Heat cooking oil. Add garlic and crab meat. Stir-fry for 1 minute.
2. Add bean sprouts, green onion, carrot, onion, pepper and salt, and stir-fry for 3 minutes.
3. Add eggs and stir-fry until eggs thicken. Remove and serve when eggs are still moist and soft.

Crab Meat with Bean Curd

Bean curd, made from soy beans, is high in protein and easily digested. When cooked with tender crab meat it makes a popular dish.

Substitution: lobster meat, shrimp

6	blocks	Bean curd, cut into cubes	6	blocks
3	Tbsp.	Cooking oil	45	mL
½	tsp.	Ginger, chopped	2	mL
¼	lb.	Crab meat	125	g
1	tsp.	Cooking wine	5	mL
½	cup	Soup stock (chicken or fish)	125	mL
1	tsp.	Salt	5	mL
1	Tbsp.	Cornstarch, dissolved in	15	mL
¼	cup	Water	60	mL
1		Egg white, beaten	1	
2	tsp.	Green onion, chopped	10	mL

1. Boil the bean curd for 1 minute. Remove and drain.
2. Heat cooking oil and stir-fry ginger and crab meat for ½ minute. Sprinkle in the wine and then add the soup stock and bean curd. Season with salt and cook for 3 minutes.
3. Add cornstarch solution. Stir gently, at the same time adding the egg white and green onion. Bring to a boil. Serve hot.

Crab Meat with Broccoli

This is a delicious low-calorie dish.

Substitution: shrimp, scallops

1	lb.	Broccoli	500	g
	dash	Salt		dash
2	Tbsp.	Cooking oil	30	mL
½	cup	Soup stock (chicken or fish)	125	mL
¼	cup	Milk	60	mL
6	oz.	Crab meat	175	g
	dash	Pepper		dash
	drops	Sesame seed oil		drops
¼	tsp.	Salt	1	mL
1	Tbsp.	Cornstarch, dissolved in	15	mL
2	Tbsp.	Water	30	mL

1. Cut broccoli tops into flowerets and stalks into thin slices.
2. To a wok filled with boiling water, add a dash of salt and the cooking oil.
3. Add broccoli and boil for 3 minutes. Drain and remove to a plate.
4. Mix soup stock with milk in a hot wok. Add crab meat, pepper, sesame seed oil, salt and boil for 1 minute.
5. Add cornstarch solution to thicken the sauce and pour over the broccoli. Serve hot.

Crab in Beer Sauce

A mellow but unusual way to combine beer with oriental cooking. Sake can be used as a substitute.

Substitution: lobster, chopped crosswise into bite-size pieces

1¾	lb.	Live crab	875	g
¼	cup	Cornstarch	60	mL
		Oil for deep-frying		
½	cup	Butter	125	mL
1	clove	Garlic, minced	1	clove
½	tsp.	Ginger, minced	2	mL
2	stalks	Green onion, cut into bite-size pieces	2	stalks
	drops	Sesame seed oil		drops
1	Tbsp.	Soy sauce	15	mL
½	tsp.	Sugar	2	mL
2	Tbsp.	Cooking wine	30	mL
½	tsp.	Salt	2	mL
1	cup	Beer	250	mL
1	Tbsp.	Cornstarch, dissolved in	15	mL
¼	cup	Water	60	mL

1. Prepare crab as in "How to Prepare Live Crab," p. 17. Divide the body into 8 to 10 sections, leaving a leg on each section. Drain for 30 minutes before cooking.
2. Use a hot wok to bring cooking to a boil.
3. Coat cut-up crab pieces with cornstarch and deep-fry for 5 minutes. Remove from oil, drain and discard oil.
4. Heat wok, melt butter and add garlic, ginger, green onion, crab, sesame seed oil, soy sauce, sugar, wine, salt and beer. Stir-fry for 1 minute. Cover and cook for another 2 minutes.
5. Add cornstarch solution and cook for 1 minute. Bring to a boil. Serve hot.

Steamed Lobster

Lobster is called "Dragon Prawn" in China, and was once considered a delicacy only for the emperor and nobleman. For those who like lobster but are calorie-conscious, steaming is the best cooking method.

Substitution: crab

2	lb.	Live lobster	1	kg
1	Tbsp.	Cooking oil	15	mL
2	stalks	Green onion, chopped	2	stalks
2	slices	Ginger, shredded	2	slices
1	tsp.	Salt	5	mL
1	tsp.	Sugar	5	mL
1/4	cup	Soup stock (chicken or fish)	60	mL
	dash	Pepper		dash
1/2	tsp.	Cornstarch, dissolved in	2	mL
1	tsp.	Water	5	mL
1	tsp.	Sesame seed oil	5	mL

1. Prepare lobster as in "How to Prepare Live Lobster," p. 18. Cut lobster in half lengthwise and then cut each half into 3 or 4 pieces. Crack the shell of the claws.
2. Steam the lobster for 20 minutes. (See "How to Steam Seafood," p. 14.)
3. Heat cooking oil in the wok. Stir-fry green onion and ginger. Add salt, sugar, soup stock and pepper. Thicken with cornstarch solution. Add sesame seed oil.
4. Pour hot sauce over lobster and serve.

Ginger Lobster

Ginger and onions give this exciting seafood delicacy a distinct flavor.

Substitution: scallops (See Ginger Crab and Ginger Oysters.)

1½	lb.	Live lobster	750	g
3	Tbsp.	Cooking oil	45	mL
6	slices	Ginger	6	slices
1	Tbsp.	Garlic, minced	15	mL
1	small	Onion, shredded	1	small
3	stalks	Green onion, cut into 3 sections	3	stalks
1	Tbsp.	Cooking wine	15	mL
2	Tbsp.	Soy sauce	30	mL
	pinch	Pepper		pinch
½	tsp.	Sugar	2	mL
	drops	Sesame seed oil		drops
1	Tbsp.	Cornstarch, dissolved in	15	mL
¼	cup	Water	60	mL

1. Prepare lobster as in "How to Prepare Live Lobster," p. 18. Chop it crosswise with the shell into small pieces.
2. Heat wok, add half the cooking oil and fry lobster. Remove.
3. Add remaining cooking oil to hot wok, then add ginger, garlic and onions. Sauté for 1 minute. Add lobster and stir-fry, then add wine, soy sauce, pepper, sugar and sesame seed oil. Cover and cook over high heat for 5 minutes.
4. Add cornstarch solution and cook for 1 minute. Serve hot.

Lobster in Blackbean Sauce

This is a spicy way to cook lobster.

Substitution: crab

1½	lb.	Live lobster	750	g
3	Tbsp.	Salted blackbeans, rinsed and drained	45	mL
1	clove	Garlic, minced	1	clove
1	Tbsp.	Ginger, minced	15	mL
1	tsp.	Cooking wine	5	mL
½	tsp.	Sugar	2	mL
3	Tbsp.	Soy sauce	45	mL
	drops	Sesame seed oil		drops
3	Tbsp.	Cooking oil	45	mL
1	Tbsp.	Cornstarch, dissolved in	15	mL
¼	cup	Water	60	mL

1. Prepare lobster as in "How to Prepare Live Lobster," p. 18. Chop it crosswise with the shell into small pieces.
2. In a bowl, combine blackbeans, garlic and ginger. Mash these ingredients into a paste, then add wine, sugar, soy sauce and sesame seed oil.
3. Heat wok, add cooking oil and fry lobster for about 5 minutes, until the shells turn to red.
4. Add blackbean mixture, stir and cover for 3 minutes.
5. Add cornstarch solution and cook until sauce thickens.

Lobster Tails
in Sweet-and-Sour Sauce

Substitution: crab

1	lb.	Lobster tails	500	g
1		Egg white	1	
1	tsp.	Cooking wine	5	mL
	drops	Sesame seed oil		drops
½	tsp.	Salt	2	mL
1	tsp.	Vinegar	5	mL
2	tsp.	Sugar	10	mL
¾	cup	Water	175	mL
¼	cup	Ketchup	60	mL
2	Tbsp.	Cornstarch	30	mL
2	Tbsp.	Cooking oil	30	mL
1		Onion, chopped fine	1	
½	cup	Green peas	125	mL

1. Remove lobster meat from shell and cut into thin slices across grain of flesh.
2. Marinate lobster in egg white, wine, sesame seed oil and salt for 30 minutes.
3. Prepare sweet-and-sour sauce, using vinegar, sugar, ⅔ of water, ketchup and cornstarch. Stir well.
4. Heat the wok, add cooking oil and onion and stir-fry for 1 minute. Add lobster slices and remaining water, cover and cook over high heat for 5 minutes.
5. Add green peas and sauce, bring to a boil and serve hot.

Lobster in Curry Sauce

A spicy way to serve whole fresh lobster. The lobster's bright orange color goes well with the color and aroma of curry.

Substitution: crab, prawn

1¾	lb.	Live lobster	875	g
¼	cup	Cornstarch	60	mL
		Salt		
		Oil for deep-frying		
3	Tbsp.	Cooking oil	45	mL
1	clove	Garlic, minced	1	clove
1	tsp.	Ginger, minced	5	mL
½	cup	Onion, shredded	125	mL
2	Tbsp.	Carrot, shredded	30	mL
2	Tbsp.	Soy sauce	30	mL
½	tsp.	Salt	2	mL
½	tsp.	Sugar	2	mL
2	tsp.	Curry powder	10	mL
¼	cup	Water	60	mL
2	Tbsp.	Coconut milk	30	mL
1	Tbsp.	Cornstarch, dissolved in	15	mL
¼	cup	Water	60	mL

1. Prepare lobster as in "How to Prepare Live Lobster," p. 18. Chop it crosswise with shell into small pieces.
2. Heat oil for deep-frying. Coat lobster pieces with cornstarch and dash of salt and deep-fry for 5 minutes. Remove lobster and discard oil.
3. Heat cooking oil. Stir-fry garlic, ginger, onion and carrot for 2 minutes. Add lobster, soy sauce, salt, sugar, coconut milk, curry powder and water. Stir-fry for 1 minute. Cover and cook for another 2 minutes.
4. Add cornstarch solution to thicken. Serve.

Lobster in Butter Sauce

Substitution: crab

1¾	lb.	Live lobster	875	g
¼	cup	Cornstarch	60	mL
		Oil for deep-frying		
½	cup	Butter	125	mL
1	clove	Garlic, minced	1	clove
½	tsp.	Ginger, minced	2	mL
2	stalks	Green onion, cut into bite-size lengths	2	stalks
	drops	Sesame seed oil		drops
2	Tbsp.	Soy sauce	30	mL
½	tsp.	Sugar	2	mL
1	Tbsp.	Cooking wine	15	mL
½	tsp.	Salt	2	mL
1	cup	Water	250	mL
1	Tbsp.	Cornstarch, dissolved in	15	mL
¼	cup	Water	60	mL

1. Prepare lobster as in "How to Prepare Live Lobster," p. 18. Chop it crosswise with shell into small pieces.
2. Use a hot wok to bring oil to a boil.
3. Coat cut-up lobster pieces in cornstarch and deep-fry for 5 minutes. Remove from oil, drain and discard oil.
4. Using high heat, melt butter in a hot wok and add garlic, ginger, green onion, lobster, sesame seed oil, soy sauce, sugar, wine, salt and water. Stir-fry for 1 minute, cover and cook for another 2 minutes.
5. Add cornstarch solution. Cook for 1 minute and bring to a boil. Serve hot.

Lobster Salad

An unusual way to use tender lobster meat. With the addition of colorful garnishes, it becomes an attractive dish for entertaining, especially since it can be prepared ahead of time.

Substitution: prawns

2	Tbsp.	Cooking oil	30	mL
1	clove	Garlic, minced	1	clove
½	cup	Coconut milk	125	mL
1		Apple, shredded	1	
½	cup	Roasted peanuts, coarsely chopped	125	mL
½	cup	Green pepper, shredded	125	mL
½	cup	Red pepper, shredded	125	mL
2	Tbsp.	Soy sauce	30	mL
½	tsp.	Salt	5	mL
1	tsp.	Sugar	5	mL
	dash	Pepper		dash
1	lb.	Lobster meat, cooked and cut into small cubes	500	g
3		Pineapple rings, cut into halves	3	
2		Tomatoes, cut into wedges	2	
3	stalks	Green onion, chopped	3	stalks

1. Heat cooking oil, add garlic and sauté for 2 minutes. Pour in coconut milk and remove from heat.
2. Finish sauce by adding apple, peanuts, red and green pepper, soy sauce, salt, sugar and pepper. Mix well.
3. Arrange lobster cubes in the center of a serving plate. Surround them with pineapple and tomato wedges. Pour the sauce over lobster. Sprinkle with chopped green onion. Chill and serve cold.

Sour Prawn Soup

Spicy and delicate, this is the most famous soup in Thailand.

Substitution: oysters, lobster tails

2	Tbsp.	Cooking oil	30	mL
2	cloves	Garlic, crushed	2	cloves
1		Lemon rind, shredded	1	
1	small	Red chili pepper, chopped	1	small
2	Tbsp.	Coriander, ground	30	mL
1	Tbsp.	Soy sauce	15	mL
1	tsp.	Salt	5	mL
¼	tsp.	Pepper	1	mL
6	cups	Soup stock (chicken or fish)	1.5	L
¾	lb.	Prawns, in the shell	375	g
1		Lemon, quartered	1	
3	stalks	Green onion, chopped fine	3	stalks

1. Heat cooking oil and stir-fry garlic. Add lemon rind, red chili pepper, coriander, soy sauce, salt, pepper and soup stock. Bring to a boil and cook for 5 minutes.
2. Add prawns and cook for 7 minutes. Squeeze in lemon juice to taste. Sprinkle with green onion. Serve.

Sesame Prawn Fingers

This dish can be prepared beforehand and is ideal for cocktail parties.

Substitution: shrimp, lobster meat

1	lb.	Prawns, shelled and deveined	500	g
½	tsp.	Sesame seed oil	2	mL
¼	tsp.	Pepper	1	mL
¼	tsp.	Salt	1	mL
1	tsp.	Cornstarch	5	mL
1-lb	loaf	Bread, cut into slices	454-g	loaf
¼	cup	Sesame seeds	60	mL
		Oil for deep-frying		
3	stalks	Green onion, chopped fine	3	stalks

1. Wash prawns and dry on paper towel.
2. Mash prawns and marinate with sesame seed oil, pepper, salt and cornstarch. Mix thoroughly.
3. Place in freezer for 30 minutes.
4. Spread mashed prawn on bread slices and sprinkle with sesame seeds.
5. Deep-fry in hot oil about 5 minutes until golden brown.
6. Cut into finger-size strips, garnish with green onion and serve with ketchup.

Cantonese Fried Prawns

This famous Chinese dish is easy to prepare.

Substitution: shrimp, lobster tails, oysters

³⁄₄	lb.	Prawns, in the shell	375	g
1	tsp.	Soy sauce	5	mL
½	tsp.	Cooking wine	2	mL
		Oil for deep-frying		
1	Tbsp.	Cooking oil	15	mL
1	tsp.	Ginger, minced	5	mL
2	tsp.	Green onion, chopped	10	mL
1	tsp.	Sugar	5	mL
	dash	Salt		dash

1. Use scissors to cut the shell at the back of each prawn and remove black vein. Wash and dry on paper towel.
2. Marinate prawns with soy sauce and cooking wine for 10 minutes.
3. Heat oil. Deep-fry prawns for 5 minutes. Remove prawns and drain oil.
4. Heat cooking oil. Stir-fry ginger and green onion for 1 minute. Add fried prawns, sugar and salt. Stir well and cook for 1 minute. Serve hot.

Crab in Beer Sauce, page 88

Spicy Fried Prawns

Great for anyone who likes it hot.

Substitution: lobster tails

1	lb.	Prawns, legs removed	500	g
		Oil for deep-frying		
1	tsp.	Ginger, minced	5	mL
1	tsp.	Green onion, chopped	5	mL
1	tsp.	Garlic, minced	5	mL
1	tsp.	Chili or Tabasco sauce	5	mL
1	tsp.	Cooking wine	5	mL
1	tsp.	Vinegar	5	mL
1	tsp.	Sugar	5	mL
1/4	tsp.	Salt	1	mL
1	tsp.	Soy sauce	5	mL
1	tsp.	Cornstarch, dissolved in	5	mL
2	Tbsp.	Water	30	mL
3	stalks	Green onion, chopped fine	3	stalks

1. Wash prawns and leave in shell. Use scissors to cut the shell at the back and devein. Cut each prawn into 2 or 3 sections.
2. Heat oil and deep-fry prawns for 1 minute. Remove prawns and leave small amount of oil in wok.
3. Add ginger, 1 tsp. chopped green onion and garlic and stir-fry for 1 minute. Then add the prawns, chili sauce, wine, vinegar, sugar, salt and soy sauce. Stir-fry for 4 minutes. Add the cornstarch solution and stir until it thickens. Arrange on plate and garnish with green onion before serving.

Sweet-and-Sour Prawns, page 106

Deep-Fried Prawns in Batter

Large prawns encased in a rich golden batter.

Substitution: shrimp

14	large	Prawns	14	large
¾	cup	Flour	175	mL
¼	tsp.	Baking powder	1	mL
1		Egg, beaten with dash of salt	1	
¾	cup	Water	175	mL
		Oil for deep-frying		

1. Shell the prawns, leaving a portion of the shell on the tail. Remove black vein from back.
2. In a bowl, combine flour, baking powder, egg and water to make batter.
3. Heat oil until it is very hot.
4. Holding the prawn by the tail, dip it in batter and gently pick it up.
5. Put the bottom (abdomen) side in the hot oil first, so that the prawn won't curl up during cooking.
6. Deep-fry about 5 minutes until golden brown. Serve immediately with plum sauce or sweet-and-sour sauce.

Prawn Cutlet

A handy dish for parties. It can be prepared well in advance.

Substitution: cod, snapper

1	lb.	Prawns	500	g
6	Tbsp.	Flour	90	mL
½	tsp.	Salt	2	mL
	dash	Pepper		dash
3		Eggs, beaten	3	
1	cup	Bread crumbs	250	mL
		Oil for deep-frying		
2		Tomatoes, sliced	2	
1		Cucumber, sliced	1	

1. Shell and devein prawns, leaving a portion of the shell on the tail.
2. Wash and dry the prawns thoroughly with paper towel.
3. Combine flour, salt and pepper. Coat prawns with flour mixture.
4. Dip prawns in beaten eggs and roll in bread crumbs.
5. Heat oil. Deep-fry prawns about 5 minutes until golden brown. Remove prawns and drain oil.
6. Garnish with tomato and cucumber. Serve with ketchup or mayonnaise.

Honey Prawns

This very special recipe is best suited for fancier gourmet meals.

Substitution: scallops, squid

1	lb.	Prawns, shelled and deveined	500	g
	dash	Salt		dash
	dash	Pepper		dash
1	Tbsp.	Cooking wine	15	mL
2	Tbsp.	Cornstarch	30	mL
⅔	cup	Flour	150	mL
1		Egg	1	
1	cup	Water	250	mL
		Oil for deep-frying		
1	Tbsp.	Cooking oil	15	mL
2	Tbsp.	Honey	30	mL
2	tsp.	Sesame seeds, toasted	10	mL

1. Wash and dry prawns.
2. Marinate prawns with salt, pepper and wine for 20 minutes.
3. Coat well with cornstarch.
4. Make a smooth batter using flour, egg and water.
5. Dip prawns in batter and deep-fry in hot oil for 5 minutes until golden brown. Remove prawns and drain on paper towel. Remove oil.
6. In a clean wok, heat cooking oil. Add honey and stir. Add the prawns and mix well. Remove to a plate, sprinkle with sesame seeds and serve hot.

Fried Prawns with Tomato Sauce

A delicate dish that is popular in China.

Substitution: lobster tails, shrimp

2	stalks	Green onion	2	stalks
1	lb.	Prawns	500	g
1	Tbsp.	Cornstarch	15	mL
2	Tbsp.	Ketchup	30	mL
¼	cup	Water	60	mL
¼	tsp.	Sugar	1	mL
1	tsp.	Soy sauce	5	mL
3	Tbsp.	Cooking oil	45	mL
4	slices	Ginger	4	slices
1	clove	Garlic, minced	1	clove
1	Tbsp.	Cooking wine	15	mL
	dash	Pepper		dash

1. Cut green onion in bite-size lengths, separating white and green parts.
2. Shells of prawns can be removed or left on. Cut the back of the shell with scissors and pull out black vein.
3. Heat the wok over high heat but use no oil. Add prawns and fry thoroughly until they turn orange. Remove and put aside.
4. Wash the wok and heat over high heat. While waiting, use a small bowl to combine cornstarch, ketchup, water, sugar and soy sauce. Stir well and set aside.
5. Put cooking oil in a hot wok. When oil begins to smoke, add ginger, garlic and white part of green onion and stir-fry for 1 minute. Add prawns, wine and pepper and stir-fry for another 2 minutes. Then pour in sauce mixture and bring to a boil. Remove to a plate, garnish with green part of green onions and serve hot.

Prawns with Cucumbers

A popular dish in our cooking classes.

Substitution: cod, red snapper, salmon

½	lb.	Prawns, shelled and deveined	250	g
	dash	Pepper		dash
	drops	Sesame seed oil		drops
1	Tbsp.	Soy sauce	15	mL
1	tsp.	Cooking wine	5	mL
6	Tbsp.	Cooking oil	90	mL
1		Cucumber, cut in half lengthwise and sliced diagonally	1	
1		Carrot, sliced diagonally	1	
1	cup	Mushrooms, cut into halves	250	mL
1	stalk	Celery, sliced diagonally	1	stalk
½	tsp.	Salt	2	mL
¼	cup	Water	60	mL
4	slices	Ginger	4	slices
2	cloves	Garlic, crushed	2	cloves
1	medium	Onion, cut into sixths	1	medium
1	Tbsp.	Cornstarch, dissolved in	15	mL
2	Tbsp.	Water	30	mL

1. Marinate prawns with pepper, sesame seed oil, soy sauce and wine for 5 minutes.
2. Heat half the cooking oil and add cucumber, carrot, mushrooms, celery, salt and water. Mix well, cover and cook for 3 minutes. Remove to a plate.
3. Heat remaining cooking oil. Add ginger, garlic and onion and stir-fry 1 minute until brown.
4. Add prawns and stir-fry until they turn orange.
5. Return all vegetables, mix well and add cornstarch solution. Stir until sauce thickens, about 30 seconds, and serve hot.

Prawns with Mushrooms

In China prawns are commonly served as part of a 10-course gourmet dinner. Chinese people have hundreds of attractive ways to cook them.

Substitution: squid, shrimp

16		Prawns, shelled and deveined	16	
1		Egg white, beaten with dash of salt	1	
1	Tbsp.	Cornstarch	15	mL
1	Tbsp.	Soy sauce	15	mL
	drops	Sesame seed oil		drops
½	cup	Water	125	mL
6	Tbsp.	Cooking oil	90	mL
1	cup	Mushrooms	250	mL
1	small	Carrot, thinly sliced	1	small
¼	tsp.	Salt	1	mL
5	slices	Ginger	5	slices
2	stalks	Green onion, cut into 3 sections	2	stalks

1. Marinate prawns with egg white for 30 minutes.
2. In a small bowl, combine cornstarch, soy sauce, sesame seed oil and half the water. Stir well and set aside.
3. Add half the cooking oil to a hot wok and wait until smoke begins to rise. Put in mushrooms, carrot, salt and remaining water. Cover and cook over high heat for 3 minutes. Remove to a plate.
4. Heat the wok and add remaining cooking oil. Add ginger and green onion and stir-fry for 30 seconds. Then add prawns and stir constantly until they curl up. Add sauce mixture and cooked mushrooms and carrot. Bring to a boil and serve hot.

Sweet-and-Sour Prawns

This very popular Chinese dish goes well with steamed rice.

Substitution: shrimp, lobster tails

¾	lb.	Prawns, shelled and deveined	375	g
½	tsp.	Cooking wine	2	mL
2	Tbsp.	Cornstarch	30	mL
		Oil for deep-frying		
2	Tbsp.	Cooking oil	30	mL
2	tsp.	Carrot, shredded and cooked	10	mL
2	tsp.	Mushrooms, sliced	10	mL
2	tsp.	Green pepper, shredded	10	mL
1	tsp.	Vinegar	5	mL
2	tsp.	Sugar	10	mL
½	tsp.	Salt	2	mL
1	tsp.	Cornstarch, dissolved in	5	mL
¼	cup	Water	60	mL
½	tsp.	Sesame seed oil	2	mL

1. Wash, dry and devein prawns.
2. Marinate prawns with wine for 10 minutes.
3. Coat prawns with cornstarch.
4. Deep-fry prawns for 10 minutes. Remove and drain oil.
5. Heat wok and add cooking oil. Stir-fry carrot, mushrooms and green pepper. Add vinegar, sugar, salt, cornstarch solution and sesame seed oil and stir.
6. Add fried prawns. Toss well and serve.

Sautéed Prawn Balls

1	lb.	Prawns	500	g
2	tsp.	Cooking wine	10	mL
¼	tsp.	Salt	1	mL
1		Egg white	1	
		Oil for deep-frying		
1	Tbsp.	Green onion, minced	15	mL
1	Tbsp.	Ginger, minced	15	mL
1		Cucumber, sliced	1	
½	tsp.	Salt	2	mL
1	Tbsp.	Cooking wine	15	mL
1	tsp.	Cornstarch, dissolved in	5	mL
¼	cup	Water	60	mL

1. Shell the prawns, leaving a portion of the shell on the tail. Devein, wash and dry with paper towel.
2. Score each prawn along the back, slicing halfway through the thickness. Cut in half crosswise.
3. Marinate prawns in wine, salt and egg white for 20 minutes.
4. Heat oil and deep-fry prawns for 10 seconds until they curl up into balls. Remove prawns.
5. Reheat wok with a little of the oil and stir-fry green onion, ginger and cucumber. Add the prawns and salt and toss with wine. Thicken with cornstarch solution. Serve hot.

Fried Prawns with Brussels Sprouts

To vary this recipe, substitute other vegetables.

Substitution: shrimp, scallops, fish

¾	lb.	Prawns, shelled and deveined	375	g
2	tsp.	Cooking wine	10	mL
1	Tbsp.	Ginger, minced	15	mL
		Oil for deep-frying		
2	Tbsp.	Cooking oil	30	mL
1	tsp.	Garlic, minced	5	mL
1	Tbsp.	Ginger, sliced	15	mL
½	cup	Carrot, sliced	125	mL
½	lb.	Brussels sprouts, cut into halves and blanched in hot water for 2 minutes	250	g
3	stalks	Green onion, chopped	3	stalks
½	cup	Soup stock (chicken or fish)	125	mL
	dash	Pepper		dash
½	tsp.	Salt	2	mL
1	tsp.	Cornstarch, dissolved in	5	mL
3	Tbsp.	Water	45	mL

1. Wash prawns and dry with paper towel.
2. Marinate prawns with wine and minced ginger for 10 minutes.
3. Heat oil for deep-frying and deep-fry prawns for 1 minute. Remove prawns and drain.
4. Heat cooking oil. Stir-fry garlic, sliced ginger, carrot and Brussels sprouts for 3 minutes. Add prawns, green onion, soup stock, pepper and salt. Bring to a boil and thicken with cornstarch solution. Serve hot.

Prawns in Blackbean Sauce

Substitution: crab, lobster tails

1	tsp.	Salted blackbeans, rinsed and drained	5	mL
1	Tbsp.	Ginger, minced	15	mL
1	clove	Garlic, minced	1	clove
3	Tbsp.	Soy sauce	45	mL
½	tsp.	Sugar	2	mL
1	tsp.	Cooking wine	5	mL
	drops	Sesame seed oil		drops
3	Tbsp.	Cooking oil	45	mL
1½	lb.	Prawns, shelled and deveined	750	g
¼	cup	Green pepper, cut into squares	60	mL
¼	cup	Red pepper, cut into squares	60	mL
1	Tbsp.	Cornstarch, dissolved in	15	mL
¼	cup	Water	60	mL

1. In a bowl, combine blackbeans, minced ginger and garlic, and mash them into a paste. Add soy sauce, sugar, wine and sesame seed oil.
2. Heat wok, add cooking oil and stir-fry prawns for about 5 minutes, until they turn orange.
3. Add blackbean mixture, green and red pepper. Mix well, cover and cook for 3 minutes.
4. Add cornstarch solution and cook until sauce thickens. Serve hot.

Prawns with Pineapple

Substitution: oysters, clams, fish

¾	lb.	Prawns, shelled and deveined	375	g
1	Tbsp.	Cornstarch	15	mL
	dash	Pepper		dash
3	Tbsp.	Cooking oil	45	mL
3	slices	Ginger, shredded	3	slices
1	clove	Garlic, minced	1	clove
2	tsp.	Soy sauce	10	mL
½	tsp.	Salt	2	mL
2	tsp.	Sugar	10	mL
1	medium	Red pepper, cut into small squares	1	medium
1	medium	Green pepper, cut into small squares	1	medium
½	cup	Carrot, sliced and cooked	125	mL
1	cup	Pineapple chunks or cubes, drained	250	mL

1. Coat prawns with a mixture of cornstarch and pepper.
2. Heat cooking oil until very hot. Stir-fry ginger and garlic for 1 minute.
3. Put in prawns, soy sauce, salt and sugar, then stir-fry for 4 minutes.
4. Add the red and green pepper, carrot and pineapple chunks. Stir-fry for another 2 minutes and serve immediately.

Butterfly Prawns

This dish is appropriate for parties as well as for the dinner table, and is a very popular dish in our restaurants. Try it with any dip.

12	large	Prawns	12	large
1	tsp.	Salt	5	mL
	dash	Pepper		dash
1	tsp.	Curry powder (optional)	5	mL
1	tsp.	Sugar	5	mL
	drops	Sesame seed oil		drops
12	slices	Bacon, cut into bite-size pieces	12	slices
2		Egg whites, lightly beaten	2	
1	cup	Bread crumbs	250	mL
2	Tbsp.	Cornstarch	30	mL
		Oil for deep-frying		

1. Remove shell from prawns, leaving a portion of the shell on the tail. Devein.
2. Using a sharp knife, slice open each prawn from the back, cutting it almost in half.
3. Marinate with salt, pepper, curry powder, sugar and sesame seed oil for 20 minutes.
4. Dip prawns and bacon in egg whites. Spread sliced prawns open flat and place a piece of bacon over each one. Coat prawns and bacon with bread crumbs mixed with cornstarch.
5. Heat oil and deep-fry prawns carefully for 5 minutes until brown.
6. Remove and drain oil.

Prawns in Satay Sauce

This traditional dish uses satay sauce, a spicy mixture of chili pepper, ginger and herbs in sesame seed oil. Originally from Southeast Asia, satay sauce is available in powder or liquid form.

Substitution: oysters, scallops, shrimp

1	lb.	Prawns, shelled and deveined	500	g
1	Tbsp.	Soy sauce	15	mL
½	tsp.	Salt	2	mL
1	tsp.	Sugar	5	mL
1	Tbsp.	Cornstarch	15	mL
	drops	Sesame seed oil		drops
3	Tbsp.	Cooking oil	45	mL
½	tsp.	Garlic, minced	2	mL
2	Tbsp.	Satay sauce	30	mL
½	cup	Onion, chopped	125	mL
1		Cucumber, sliced	1	

1. Wash and dry prawns.
2. Marinate with soy sauce, salt, sugar, cornstarch and sesame seed oil for 20 minutes.
3. Heat cooking oil. Stir-fry garlic for 15 seconds, then add prawns and stir-fry for 5 minutes. Add satay sauce and chopped onion. Continue to stir-fry for another 3 minutes. Remove to plate. Garnish with sliced cucumber. Serve hot with steamed rice.

Skewered Prawns

This dish is ideal for parties because it can be prepared well ahead. It is very popular in Southeast Asia.

Substitution: scallops, oysters, clams

1	lb.	Prawns, shelled and deveined	500	g
1	Tbsp.	Soy sauce	15	mL
1	Tbsp.	Cornstarch	15	mL
2	tsp.	Sugar	10	mL
8	small	Bamboo skewers	8	small
		Oil for deep-frying		
1	small	Cucumber, sliced	1	small
¼	cup	Satay sauce	60	mL

1. Wash and dry prawns.
2. Marinate in soy sauce, cornstarch and sugar for 20 minutes.
3. Put prawns on bamboo skewers.
4. Deep-fry skewered prawns in hot oil for 5 minutes.
5. Remove from oil and drain on paper towel.
6. Serve with sliced cucumber and satay sauce.

Garlic Prawns

Substitution: clams, oysters

12		Prawns, in the shell	12	
½	cup	Garlic, minced	125	mL
2	Tbsp.	Cooking oil	30	mL
1	Tbsp.	Soy sauce	15	mL
	dash	Pepper		dash
¼	tsp.	Sugar	1	mL
2	Tbsp.	Green onion, chopped	30	mL

1. Wash and dry prawns. Cut them into halves lengthwise. Arrange on a plate with the meat side up. Sprinkle half of minced garlic on top.
2. Steam prawns in wok for 5 minutes. (See "How to Steam Seafood," p. 14.) Remove and keep warm.
3. Heat cooking oil and add remaining garlic. When oil is smoking hot, spoon the garlic and oil over the prawns. Add soy sauce, pepper, sugar and chopped green onion, toss and serve hot.

Prawns in Coconut Sauce

This dish is popular in Thailand, where coconuts are plentiful. It has a fragrant aroma.

Substitution: shrimp, fish, scallops

12	large	Prawns	12	large
1/4	tsp.	Salt	1	mL
1/4	tsp.	Pepper	1	mL
3	Tbsp.	Cooking oil	45	mL
2	slices	Ginger, shredded	2	slices
1	large	Onion, chopped fine	1	large
1	large	Tomato, chopped fine	1	large
1		Red chili pepper, shredded (optional)	1	
2	Tbsp.	Soy sauce	30	mL
1	tsp.	Sugar	5	mL
1	cup	Coconut milk, thick	250	mL

1. Remove shell from prawns, leaving a portion of the shell on the tail. Slit prawns down the back and devein. Sprinkle with salt and pepper and set aside for 5 minutes.
2. Heat cooking oil. Stir-fry ginger, onion, tomato and red chili pepper for 2 minutes. Add soy sauce, sugar and coconut milk. Cook over low heat for 2 minutes.
3. Add prawns and cook for another 5 minutes. Serve with steamed rice.

Colorful Shrimp Soup

Popular in our restaurants, this soup uses wonton wrappers cut into tiny squares and deep-fried.

Substitution: crab, clams, small oysters

3	cups	Soup stock (chicken or fish)	750	mL
6	oz.	Shrimp meat, raw	175	g
1/4	cup	Carrots, diced	60	mL
2	Tbsp.	Green peas	30	mL
1/4	cup	Bamboo shoots, diced	60	mL
3	Tbsp.	Mushrooms, sliced	45	mL
	dash	Pepper		dash
1/2	tsp.	Salt	2	mL
1/2	tsp.	Cooking wine	2	mL
2	Tbsp.	Cornstarch, dissolved in	30	mL
1/4	cup	Water	60	mL
1		Egg white, beaten	1	
1	Tbsp.	Green onion	15	mL
2	Tbsp.	Wonton wrapper squares, deep-fried (optional)	30	mL

1. Bring soup stock to a boil.
2. Add shrimp, carrots, peas, bamboo shoots, mushrooms, pepper, salt and wine. Boil for 5 minutes.
3. Add cornstarch solution and bring to a boil. Stir in egg white in a circular motion.
4. Sprinkle with green onion and wonton squares. Serve hot.

Shrimp Fried Rice

Substitution: crab meat, fish fillets

1	cup	Shrimp, shelled and deveined	250	mL
1	tsp.	Cooking wine	5	mL
	dash	Pepper		dash
1/4	tsp.	Salt	1	mL
2	Tbsp.	Cooking oil	30	mL
4	cups	Cooked rice, cold	1	L
2	large	Eggs, beaten with dash of salt	2	large
2	Tbsp.	Soy sauce	30	mL
2	stalks	Green onion, chopped fine	2	stalks
1	cup	Green peas	250	mL

1. Marinate shrimp with wine, pepper and salt in a wok for 5 minutes.
2. Heat cooking oil and stir-fry shrimp until cooked.
3. Add rice and stir constantly for 5 minutes until the rice is hot. Add salt to taste and gently pour eggs over the rice. Stir for another 2 minutes, add soy sauce, green onion and green peas. Stir-fry for 1 minute and serve hot.

Coconut Shrimp Balls

A fragrant way to prepare minced shrimp meat. Excellent as an hors d'oeuvre.

Substitution: crab meat

1	lb.	Shrimp, shelled and deveined	500	g
2		Eggs	2	
¼	cup	Coconut, grated	60	mL
2	Tbsp.	Cornstarch	30	mL
3	Tbsp.	Green onion, chopped fine	45	mL
3	Tbsp.	Water chestnut, chopped fine	45	mL
½	tsp.	Salt	2	mL
		Oil for deep-frying		
4	cups	Fresh bread cubes	1	L
¼	tsp.	Pepper	1	mL
½	tsp.	Cooking wine	2	mL
	drops	Sesame seed oil		drops

1. Finely chop shrimp and mix with remaining ingredients, except oil and bread cubes. Refrigerate for 30 minutes.
2. Using a teaspoonful of mixture at a time, shape into small balls.
3. Coat balls with bread cubes.
4. Deep-fry in hot oil for 5 minutes. Remove and drain oil. Serve with a sweet-and-sour sauce or any other dip.

Fried Shrimp Rolls

Prepared with a minimum of fat and a maximum of flavor, Fried Shrimp Rolls make an excellent hors d'oeuvre and can be used with any dip.

Substitution: crab, prawns, lobster

¼	tsp.	Salt	1	mL
¾	lb.	Shrimp, shelled and deveined	375	g
½	tsp.	Cooking wine	2	mL
	dash	Pepper		dash
1		Egg white	1	
1	Tbsp.	Cornstarch	15	mL
	drops	Sesame seed oil		drops
10	slices	White sandwich bread, crust removed	10	slices
		Oil for deep-frying		
1	Tbsp.	Green onion, minced	15	mL

1. Add salt and mash shrimp into fine paste. Put in a bowl with wine, pepper, egg white, cornstarch and sesame seed oil.
2. Using a spoon, stir solution in a single continuous direction for 2 minutes until it thickens.
3. Divide paste into 10 portions and spread on bread slices, then roll up jelly-roll style. Secure with bamboo skewer if necessary.
4. Cut each roll in 2, heat oil and deep-fry about 3 minutes or until golden brown. Sprinkle with green onion and serve.

Shrimp with Cashew Nuts

Substitution: clams, squid, prawns

¾	lb.	Shrimp, shelled and deveined	375	g
½	tsp.	Salt	2	mL
	dash	Pepper		dash
1	Tbsp.	Soy sauce	15	mL
2	tsp.	Sugar	10	mL
1	Tbsp.	Cooking wine	15	mL
	drops	Sesame seed oil		drops
3	Tbsp.	Cooking oil	45	mL
2	slices	Ginger, shredded	2	slices
1	clove	Garlic, chopped	1	clove
½	cup	Cashew nuts, roasted	125	mL
¼	cup	Peas	60	mL
1	tsp.	Cornstarch, dissolved in	5	mL
3	Tbsp.	Water	45	mL

1. Wash and dry shrimp.
2. Marinate with salt, pepper, soy sauce, sugar, wine and sesame seed oil for 20 minutes.
3. Heat cooking oil and stir-fry ginger and garlic.
4. Add shrimp and stir-fry for 3 minutes.
5. Add cashew nuts and peas and continue to stir-fry for another 2 minutes. Add cornstarch solution and bring to a boil. Serve immediately.

Shrimp Foo Young

A very popular wok dish, Shrimp Foo Young can be served at dinner or at breakfast.

Substitution: crab meat, small oysters

½	lb.	Shrimp	250	g
3	Tbsp.	Cooking oil	45	mL
1	cup	Bean sprouts	250	mL
¼	cup	Green pepper, slivered	60	mL
¼	cup	Carrots, slivered	60	mL
2	Tbsp.	Green onion, chopped	30	mL
	dash	Pepper		dash
½	tsp.	Salt	2	mL
	drops	Sesame seed oil		drops
5	large	Eggs, beaten with dash of salt	5	large

1. Peel shell from shrimp and make a slit lengthwise down the back. Remove black vein, wash and drain.
2. Heat cooking oil and add shrimp. Stir-fry for 2 minutes.
3. Add sprouts, green pepper, carrots, green onion, pepper, salt and sesame seed oil. Add eggs. Stir-fry until eggs thicken but are still moist. Serve hot.

Wok and Rolls

An original creation, Wok and Rolls can be served as an hors d'oeuvre or as a light entrée.

Substitution: crab, prawns

1		Egg	1	
1		Egg yolk	1	
	dash	Salt		dash
1	tsp.	Cornstarch	5	mL
2	tsp.	Water	10	mL
¾	lb.	Shrimp, shelled and deveined	375	g
½	tsp.	Salt	2	mL
2	tsp.	Cooking wine	10	mL
	dash	Pepper		dash
2	large	Romaine lettuce leaves, washed and dried	2	large
4	thin	Carrot sticks, parboiled	4	thin
1	tsp.	Cornstarch, dissolved in	5	mL
1	tsp.	Water to make a paste	5	mL

1. In a bowl, thoroughly beat egg and egg yolk, dash of salt, cornstarch and water.
2. Wipe surface of a clean wok with oil-soaked paper.
3. Pour in egg mixture and cook over low heat. Rotate the wok to make the solution spread evenly to form a thin sheet. When egg is set, remove to cutting board.
4. Mash shrimp into a paste using the flat side of a cleaver. Put paste in a bowl, mix with salt, wine and pepper and stir in one direction continuously for 2 minutes until sticky.
5. Trim the edges of the egg sheet to make a square. Cooked surface should be face-up.
6. Dust the surface with cornstarch. Spread half of the shrimp paste evenly on the egg sheet.
7. Place lettuce leaves on top, then cover with the rest of the shrimp paste.
8. Arrange 2 carrot sticks on two opposite sides of the square. Roll the egg

sheet over the carrots from both sides toward the center until the ends meet. Brush the seam with cornstarch paste.

9. Place the roll seam-downward on a lightly greased plate and steam over high heat for 10 minutes. (See "How to Steam Seafood," p. 14.) Cut into sections and serve hot.

Stir-Fried Shrimp with Vegetables

Substitution: prawns, scallops

³⁄₄	lb.	Shrimp	375	g
	dash	Pepper		dash
¹⁄₂	tsp.	Cooking wine	2	mL
	dash	Salt		dash
2	Tbsp.	Cooking oil	30	mL
¹⁄₂	tsp.	Garlic, minced	2	mL
¹⁄₂	tsp.	Ginger, minced	2	mL
1	cup	Broccoli flowerets	250	mL
¹⁄₂	cup	Snow peas, strings removed	125	mL
¹⁄₄	cup	Carrot, sliced	60	mL
1		Onion, cut into wedges	1	
¹⁄₄	tsp.	Salt	1	mL
1	cup	Soup stock (chicken or fish)	250	mL
¹⁄₂	tsp.	Soy sauce	2	mL
	drops	Sesame seed oil		drops
¹⁄₂	tsp.	Sugar	2	mL
1	tsp.	Cornstarch, dissolved in	5	mL
2	Tbsp.	Water	30	mL

1. Marinate shrimp with pepper, wine and a dash of salt. Refrigerate for 20 minutes.
2. Heat cooking oil and add garlic, ginger and shrimp and stir-fry until shrimp is pink.
3. Add all vegetables and salt and stir-fry for 1 minute. Add soup stock, cover and cook over high heat for 3 minutes, until steam escapes from edge of lid.
4. Stir in soy sauce, sesame seed oil, sugar and cornstarch solution and cook until thickened. Serve hot.

Shrimp Almond Ding

Substitution: prawns, scallops

1	lb.	Shrimp	500	g
1	Tbsp.	Soy sauce	15	mL
1	tsp.	Cornstarch	5	mL
	drops	Sesame seed oil		drops
	dash	Salt		dash
3	Tbsp.	Cooking oil	45	mL
½	tsp.	Garlic, minced	2	mL
½	tsp.	Ginger, minced	2	mL
3	stalks	Green onion, cut into 3 pieces	3	stalks
3	stalks	Celery, diced	3	stalks
½	cup	Bamboo shoots, diced	125	mL
½	cup	Mushrooms, diced	125	mL
½	cup	Carrot, diced	125	mL
½	cup	Green pepper, diced	125	mL
2	tsp.	Cooking wine	10	mL
½	tsp.	Salt	2	mL
½	tsp.	Sugar	2	mL
1	tsp.	Cornstarch, dissolved in	5	mL
¼	cup	Water	60	mL
½	cup	Almonds, toasted	125	mL

1. Peel shrimp and make a slit lengthwise down the back. Remove black vein, wash and drain.
2. Marinate shrimp with soy sauce, cornstarch, sesame seed oil and a dash of salt. Refrigerate for 15 minutes.
3. Heat cooking oil. Add garlic, ginger and green onion and stir-fry for 20 seconds until brown. Then add shrimp and stir-fry for 3 minutes.
4. Add celery, bamboo shoots, mushrooms, carrots, green pepper, wine, salt and sugar. Sauté over high heat for 3 minutes.
5. Add cornstarch solution to wok. Bring to a boil. Add toasted almonds, mix and serve.

Steamed Shrimp

An easy way to enjoy the delicate flavor of shrimp, this dish is very popular in Southeast Asia, especially for festive occasions.

Substitution: prawns

1	lb.	Shrimp, in the shell	500	g
2	tsp.	Cooking wine	10	mL
½	tsp.	Salt	2	mL
2	stalks	Green onion, finely chopped	2	stalks
2	slices	Ginger, minced	2	slices

1. Wash shrimp and drain.
2. Marinate shrimp with wine, salt, green onion and ginger for 20 minutes.
3. Put shrimp on a plate and steam for 3 minutes. (See "How to Steam Seafood," p. 14.) Turn off heat and let stand for 1 minute.
4. Serve hot with mustard sauce or any sauce of your choice.

Hot Mustard Shrimp

For anyone who likes it hot and likes to be adventurous, this is the dish. Instead of deep-frying, you can grill these kabobs on an hibachi, turning frequently.

Substitution: prawns, oysters

1	lb.	Shrimp, medium-size	500	g
3	Tbsp.	Mustard powder	45	mL
¼	tsp.	Salt	1	mL
1	tsp.	Sugar	5	mL
1	tsp.	Horseradish	5	mL
½	cup	Flat beer or water	125	mL
¼	tsp.	Sesame seed oil	1	mL
8	small	Bamboo skewers	8	small
1		Green pepper, cut into small squares	1	
1		Red pepper, cut into small squares	1	
1	small	Onion, cut into wedges	1	small
		Oil for deep-frying		

1. Remove shell and legs from shrimp, devein, wash and dry on paper towel.
2. In a bowl, mix mustard powder, salt, sugar, horseradish and beer or water into a paste first, then gently into a very thin sauce.
3. Add the sesame seed oil and dip shrimp into the mixture.
4. Skewer the shrimp with pepper and onion pieces.
5. Deep-fry in hot oil for 4 minutes.

Shrimp Chop Suey

Substitution: prawns, lobster meat

½	lb.	Shrimp, shelled and deveined	250	g
	dash	Salt		dash
6	Tbsp.	Cooking oil	90	mL
2	stalks	Celery, sliced diagonally	2	stalks
2		Carrots, sliced diagonally	2	
½	cup	Waterchestnuts	125	mL
1		Green pepper, cut into small squares	1	
½	lb.	Bean sprouts	250	g
½	cup	Bamboo shoots, shredded	125	mL
½	tsp.	Salt	2	mL
3	slices	Ginger	3	slices
1		Onion, shredded	1	
1	Tbsp.	Cornstarch, dissolved in	15	mL
½	cup	Water	125	mL
1½	Tbsp.	Soy sauce	25	mL

1. Sprinkle shrimp with salt.
2. Heat half the cooking oil. Add celery, carrots, waterchestnuts, green pepper, bean sprouts, bamboo shoots and salt. Cover and cook for 3 minutes. Remove to a dish.
3. Add remaining cooking oil to hot wok, then ginger, onion and shrimp and stir-fry for 2 minutes. Add cornstarch solution and soy sauce and bring to a boil. Return all vegetables to wok, mix and serve hot.

Mother and Daughter Shrimp

Substitution: lobster

1	lb.	Shrimp, peeled and deveined	500	g
1		Egg white	1	
1	Tbsp.	Cornstarch	15	mL
½	tsp.	Salt	2	mL
2	Tbsp.	Cooking oil	30	mL
2-4	stalks	Green onion, cut into bite-size pieces	2-4	stalks
1	Tbsp.	Ginger, slivered	15	mL
1	Tbsp.	Cooking wine	15	mL
1	cup	Broccoli flowerets, cut into bite-size pieces and blanched	250	mL
	drops	Sesame seed oil		drops
3-4	Tbsp.	Ketchup	45-60	mL
½	tsp.	Sugar	2	mL

1. Clean shrimp and pat dry on paper towel.
2. Marinate shrimp in egg white, cornstarch and salt for 10 minutes.
3. Arrange broccoli in a row down the center of a platter.
4. Heat cooking oil and add green onion and ginger. Stir-fry for 15 seconds, then add shrimp, wine and sesame seed oil. Stir for 3 minutes until shrimp turn orange. Remove half the shrimp mixture and place on one side of the platter.
5. Add ketchup and sugar to the wok and fry the rest of the shrimp for 1 minute. Place on the other side of the platter. Serve hot.

Mollusks

Abalone with Vegetables

Abalone, very delicate and lean, is commonly served in 10-course gourmet dinners in China.

Substitution: squid, shrimp, prawns

1	Tbsp.	Cornstarch	15	mL
1	Tbsp.	Soy sauce	15	mL
	drops	Sesame seed oil		drops
½	tsp.	Sugar	2	mL
6	Tbsp.	Cooking oil	90	mL
1	cup	Mushrooms, cut into halves	250	mL
1	small	Carrot, sliced thin	1	small
1	cup	Celery, cut into bite-size pieces	250	mL
¼	tsp.	Salt	1	mL
¼	cup	Water	60	mL
5	slices	Ginger	5	slices
2	stalks	Green onion, cut into bite-size lengths	2	stalks
¾	lb.	Abalone meat, sliced thin	375	g

1. Combine cornstarch, soy sauce, sesame seed oil and sugar in small bowl. Stir well.
2. Heat half of cooking oil until smoke begins to rise. Add mushrooms, carrot, celery, salt and water. Cover and cook for 3 minutes. Remove to a plate.
3. Heat remaining cooking oil. Add ginger and green onion and stir-fry for 30 seconds, then add abalone slices and stir-fry for 4 minutes. Add sauce and mushroom mixture. Bring to a boil and serve hot.

Hors d'Oeuvres: Wok and Rolls, page 122
Coconut Shrimp Balls, page 118
Sesame Prawn Fingers, page 97
Stuffed Crab Claws, page 77

Abalone with Oyster Sauce

In the Orient, this dish is reserved for special celebrations. Oyster sauce is a thick, brown sauce made from oysters, soy sauce and brine and is available in specialty shops and supermarkets.

¼	cup	Cooking oil	60	mL
1	cup	Broccoli flowerets, cut into bite-size pieces	250	mL
½	tsp.	Salt	2	mL
2	slices	Ginger	2	slices
½	tsp.	Cooking wine	2	mL
½	tsp.	Garlic, minced	2	mL
¾	lb.	Abalone, sliced thin	375	g
2	Tbsp.	Oyster sauce	30	mL
1	tsp.	Sugar	5	mL
	drops	Sesame seed oil		drops
1	Tbsp.	Soy sauce	15	mL
1	Tbsp.	Cornstarch, dissolved in	15	mL
¼	cup	Water	60	mL

1. Heat half the cooking oil until very hot. Add broccoli, salt, ginger and wine; stir-fry for 3 minutes. Remove to a platter.
2. Heat remaining cooking oil until very hot. Add garlic and abalone and stir-fry for 5 minutes.
3. In a bowl, combine oyster sauce, sugar, sesame seed oil, soy sauce and cornstarch solution. Add to wok and bring to a boil.
4. Arrange abalone on top of broccoli. Serve hot.

Squid with Vegetables, page 151

Steamed Clams

Substitution: mussels

2	lb.	Clams	1	Kg
2	Tbsp.	Soy sauce	30	mL
¼	tsp.	Sesame seed oil	2	mL
	dash	Pepper		dash
2	slices	Ginger, shredded	2	slices

1. Clean the clamshells with a brush.
2. Steam clams for 5 minutes until all the shells are open. (See "How to Steam Seafood," p. 14.)
3. Serve with a dip made from a mixture of soy sauce, sesame seed oil, pepper and shredded ginger.

Clams in Butter Sauce

Atlantic clams are more suitable for this recipe because the shells are softer. Smooth butter sauce complements the distinctive flavor of clams.

Substitution: lobster, crab, scallops

2	lb.	Clams	1	Kg
½	cup	Butter	125	mL
1	clove	Garlic, minced	1	clove
½	tsp.	Ginger, minced	2	mL
2	stalks	Green onion, cut into bite-size pieces	2	stalks
	drops	Sesame seed oil		drops
2	Tbsp.	Soy sauce	30	mL
½	tsp.	Sugar	2	mL
1	Tbsp.	Cooking wine	15	mL
½	tsp.	Salt	2	mL
¼	cup	Water	60	mL
5	tsp.	Cornstarch, dissolved in	25	mL
¼	cup	Water	60	mL

1. In a wok filled with enough boiling water to cover clams, boil them until shells open. Remove and drain.
2. Use high heat to melt butter in wok. Add garlic, ginger, green onion, sesame seed oil, soy sauce, sugar, wine, salt, water and clams. Stir-fry for 1 minute. Cover and cook for another 2 minutes.
3. Add cornstarch solution. Cook for 1 minute. Bring to a boil. Serve hot.

Clams in Ginger and Onion Sauce

Substitution: scallops, oysters

2	lb.	Clams	1	Kg
3	Tbsp.	Cooking oil	45	mL
1	Tbsp.	Garlic, minced	15	mL
6	slices	Ginger	6	slices
1	small	Onion, shredded	1	small
1	Tbsp.	Cooking wine	15	mL
3	stalks	Green onion, chopped	3	stalks
2	Tbsp.	Soy sauce	30	mL
	dash	Pepper		dash
½	tsp.	Sugar	2	mL
	drops	Sesame seed oil		drops
5	tsp.	Cornstarch, dissolved in	25	mL
¼	cup	Water	60	mL

1. In a wok filled with enough boiling water to cover clams, boil them until shells open. Remove and drain.
2. Heat cooking oil. Add garlic, ginger and onion and sauté for 1 minute. Add clams and stir-fry.
3. Add wine, green onion, soy sauce, pepper, sugar and sesame seed oil. Cover and cook for 5 minutes.
4. Add cornstarch solution and cook for 1 minute. Mix well and serve hot.

Clams in Satay Sauce

Substitution: oysters, shrimp, squid

3	Tbsp.	Cooking oil	45	mL
1/2	tsp.	Garlic, minced	2	mL
1/2	tsp.	Ginger, shredded	2	mL
1/4	cup	Onion, shredded	60	mL
3/4	lb.	Clam meat, cooked	375	g
1	Tbsp.	Satay sauce	15	mL
2	Tbsp.	Water	30	mL
1/2	tsp.	Salt	2	mL
1	Tbsp.	Carrot, sliced and cooked	15	mL
1/4	cup	Green peas	60	mL
1	tsp.	Cornstarch, dissolved in	5	mL
1/4	cup	Water	60	mL
1	tsp.	Soy sauce	5	mL
	drops	Sesame seed oil		drops
2	stalks	Green onion, chopped fine	2	stalks
10	slices	Cucumber	10	slices

1. Heat cooking oil. Stir-fry garlic, ginger and onion for 1 minute.
2. Add clam meat, satay sauce, water, salt, carrot and green peas. Stir-fry for 2 minutes.
3. Add cornstarch solution, soy sauce and sesame seed oil and bring to a boil.
4. Remove to a plate. Sprinkle with chopped green onion, and garnish with cucumber slices. Serve hot.

Clams in Blackbean Sauce

Substitution: crab, scallops, shrimp

2	lb.	Clams	1	Kg
3	Tbsp.	Salted blackbeans, rinsed and drained	45	mL
1	Tbsp.	Ginger, minced	15	mL
2	tsp.	Garlic, minced	10	mL
3	Tbsp.	Soy sauce	45	mL
1	Tbsp.	Cooking wine	15	mL
½	tsp.	Sugar	2	mL
1		Red chili pepper, shredded (optional)	1	
	drops	Sesame seed oil		drops
3	Tbsp.	Cooking oil	45	mL
5	tsp.	Cornstarch, dissolved in	25	mL
¼	cup	Water	60	mL

1. In a wok filled with enough boiling water to cover clams, boil them until shells open. Drain water.
2. In a bowl, mash blackbeans, ginger and garlic into a paste. Add soy sauce, wine, sugar, red chili pepper and sesame seed oil.
3. Heat wok, add cooking oil and stir-fry clams for about 5 minutes.
4. Add blackbean mixture. Mix well, cover and cook for 3 minutes.
5. Add cornstarch solution. Cook until sauce thickens. Serve hot.

Deep-Fried Oysters

Substitution: clams

12		Oysters, shucked	12	
1	tsp.	Salt	5	mL
1	cup	Flour	250	mL
¼	tsp.	Baking powder	1	mL
1	large	Egg	1	large
¾	cup	Water or beer	175	mL
		Oil for deep-frying		
1	cup	Shredded lettuce	250	mL
½		Lemon, cut into 3 sections	½	

1. Clean oysters by gently mixing them with salted water. Wash under cold running water and drain.
2. In a wok filled with enough boiling water to cover oysters, boil them for 2 minutes. Remove to a strainer and allow to dry for 30 minutes.
3. In a bowl, combine flour, baking powder, egg and water or beer. Mix well.
4. Dip oysters one at a time in batter, then deep-fry in hot oil for 5 minutes until golden brown.
5. Place on shredded lettuce and serve with lemon sections.

Ginger Oysters

Ginger eliminates the fishy aroma and adds an appetizing flavor to any seafood.

Substitution: scallops (See Ginger Crab and Ginger Lobster.)

1½	lb.	Oysters	750	g
½	tsp.	Salt	2	mL
1	tsp.	Ginger, minced	5	mL
3	Tbsp.	Cooking wine	45	mL
3	Tbsp.	Cooking oil	45	mL
6	slices	Ginger	6	slices
1	small	Onion, shredded	1	small
3	stalks	Green onion, cut into 3 pieces	3	stalks
1	Tbsp.	Garlic, minced	15	mL
2	Tbsp.	Soy sauce	30	mL
	dash	Pepper		dash
½	tsp.	Sugar	2	mL
	drops	Sesame seed oil		drops
1	Tbsp.	Cornstarch, dissolved in	15	mL
¼	cup	Water	60	mL

1. Clean oysters by gently mixing them with salted water. Wash under cold running water and drain. Marinate with minced ginger and 2/3 of the wine.
2. In a wok filled with enough boiling water to cover oysters, boil them for 30 seconds. Remove and drain.
3. Heat cooking oil, add sliced ginger, onions and garlic and sauté for 1 minute. Add oysters and stir-fry, then add remaining wine, soy sauce, pepper, sugar and sesame seed oil. Cover and cook for 5 minutes.
4. Add cornstarch solution and cook for 1 minute. Serve hot.

Oysters in Blackbean Sauce

Substitution: crab, lobster

3	Tbsp.	Salted blackbeans, rinsed and drained	45	mL
1	clove	Garlic, minced	1	clove
1	Tbsp.	Ginger, minced	15	mL
1	tsp.	Cooking wine	2	mL
½	tsp.	Sugar	45	mL
3	Tbsp.	Soy sauce	45	mL
	drops	Sesame seed oil		drops
1½	lb.	Oysters	750	g
3	Tbsp.	Cooking oil	45	mL
1	Tbsp.	Cornstarch, dissolved in	15	mL
¼	cup	Water	60	mL

1. In a bowl, crush blackbeans, garlic and ginger into a paste. Then add wine, sugar, soy sauce and sesame seed oil.
2. Clean oysters by gently mixing them with salted water. Rinse under cold running water and drain.
3. In a wok filled with enough boiling water to cover oysters, boil them for 1 minute. Remove and drain.
4. Heat cooking oil and stir-fry oysters for 1 minute.
5. Add blackbean mixture, mix well, cover and cook for 3 minutes.
6. Add cornstarch solution and cook until sauce thickens. Serve hot.

Oyster Foo Young

Substitution: crab meat, shrimp

½	lb.	Oysters, shucked	250	g
3	Tbsp.	Cooking oil	45	mL
1	Tbsp.	Ginger, minced	15	mL
1	cup	Bean sprouts	250	mL
¼	cup	Green pepper, slivered	60	mL
2	Tbsp.	Green onion, chopped	30	mL
¼	cup	Carrot, slivered	60	mL
	dash	Pepper		dash
¼	cup	Onion, shredded	60	mL
½	tsp.	Salt	2	mL
	drops	Sesame seed oil		drops
5	large	Eggs, beaten with dash of salt	5	large

1. Clean oysters by gently mixing them with salted water. Rinse under cold running water and drain.
2. In a wok filled with enough boiling water to cover oysters, boil them for 2 minutes. Remove and drain.
3. Heat cooking oil. Add ginger and oysters and stir-fry for 2 minutes.
4. Add bean sprouts, green pepper, green onion, carrot, pepper, onion, salt and sesame seed oil. Add eggs and stir-fry until eggs thicken. Remove and serve when eggs are still moist and soft.

Oysters with Mushrooms

Substitution: shrimp, scallops, crab

10	oz.	Oysters, shucked	300	mL
1	tsp.	Ginger, minced	5	mL
1	Tbsp.	Cooking wine	15	mL
3	Tbsp.	Cooking oil	45	mL
6	slices	Ginger, sliced thin	6	slices
2	stalks	Green onion, cut into short lengths	2	stalks
½		Red chili pepper, shredded	½	
½	cup	Mushrooms, sliced	125	mL
½	cup	Cucumber, shredded	125	mL
1	tsp.	Salt	5	mL
1	tsp.	Soy sauce	5	mL
2	tsp.	Cornstarch, dissolved in	10	mL
4	tsp.	Water	20	mL
	drops	Sesame seed oil		drops

1. Clean oysters by gently mixing them with salted water. Rinse under cold running water, drain and dry.
2. Add minced ginger and wine and marinate for 20 minutes.
3. In a wok filled with enough boiling water to cover oysters, boil them for 2 minutes.
4. Heat cooking oil. Add sliced ginger, green onion and red chili pepper. Stir-fry for 1 minute. Add mushrooms, cucumber, oysters, salt and soy sauce.
5. Thicken with cornstarch solution. Sprinkle with sesame seed oil and toss. Serve immediately.

Scallops with Cauliflower

Substitution: clams

6	Tbsp.	Cooking oil	90	mL
4	slices	Ginger	4	slices
1	large	Cauliflower, cut into bite-size pieces	1	large
1		Carrot, sliced diagonally	1	
1	stalk	Celery, sliced diagonally	1	stalk
½	tsp.	Salt	2	mL
¼	cup	Water	60	mL
2	cloves	Garlic, crushed	2	cloves
¾	lb.	Scallops	375	g
1	Tbsp.	Soy sauce	15	mL
¼	tsp.	Sugar	1	mL
	dash	Pepper		dash
	drops	Sesame seed oil		drops
1	tsp.	Cooking wine	5	mL
1	tsp.	Cornstarch, dissolved in	5	mL
¼	cup	Water	60	mL

1. Heat half the cooking oil and add ginger. Stir-fry for 1 minute until brown, then add cauliflower, carrot, celery, salt and water. Stir and cover. Cook for 5 minutes and remove to a plate.
2. Add remaining cooking oil to a hot wok and add garlic. Brown for 30 seconds and add scallops. Stir-fry for 4 minutes. Add soy sauce, sugar, pepper, sesame seed oil, wine and cornstarch solution. Bring to a boil and return vegetables. Mix well and serve hot.

Scallops with Snow Peas

Substitution: squid, shrimp, prawns

good

1	lb.	Scallops	500	g
1	Tbsp.	Cornstarch	15	mL
1	Tbsp.	Soy sauce	15	mL
	drops	Sesame seed oil		drops
6	Tbsp.	Cooking oil	90	mL
½	tsp.	Garlic, minced	2	mL
5	slices	Ginger	5	slices
½	lb.	Snow peas	250	g
1	small	Carrot, sliced thin	1	small
¼	tsp.	Salt	1	mL
¼	cup	Water	60	mL
2	stalks	Green onion, cut into 3 pieces	2	stalks

1. Wash scallops and drain for 30 minutes.
2. Combine cornstarch, soy sauce and sesame seed oil in a small bowl. Stir well.
3. Add half the cooking oil to a hot wok and wait until smoke begins to rise. Add garlic and ginger and brown for 30 seconds, then add snow peas, carrot, salt and water. Stir-fry for 3 minutes. Remove to a plate.
4. Heat remaining cooking oil. Add green onion and stir-fry for 30 seconds. Then add scallops and stir-fry constantly for about 4 minutes.
5. Return snow pea mixture and add sauce mixture. Bring to a boil and serve hot.

Fried Scallops with Vegetables

You can use almost any vegetable as a substitute for broccoli. Green beans are especially good, or a combination of zucchini and mushrooms.

Substitution: shrimp

1	lb.	Scallops	500	g
2	tsp.	Cooking wine	10	mL
1	Tbsp.	Ginger, minced	15	mL
		Oil for deep-frying		
2	Tbsp.	Cooking oil	30	mL
1	tsp.	Garlic, minced	5	mL
1	Tbsp.	Ginger, sliced	15	mL
½	cup	Carrot, sliced	125	mL
½	lb.	Broccoli, cut into	250	g
		small pieces		
3	stalks	Green onion, chopped	3	stalks
½	cup	Soup stock (chicken or fish)	125	mL
½	tsp.	Salt	2	mL
	dash	Pepper		dash
1	tsp.	Cornstarch, dissolved in	5	mL
3	Tbsp.	Water	45	mL

1. Wash scallops and dry with paper towel.
2. Marinate scallops with wine and minced ginger for 10 minutes.
3. Heat oil for deep-frying and deep-fry scallops for 1 minute. Remove scallops and drain oil.
4. Heat cooking oil. Stir-fry garlic, sliced ginger, carrot and broccoli for 2 minutes. Add scallops, green onion, soup stock, salt and pepper. Bring to a boil and thicken with cornstarch solution. Serve hot with steamed rice.

Scallops in Satay Sauce

This spicy dish is very popular in the East.

Substitution: prawns, clams, squid

1	lb.	Scallops	500	g
1	tsp.	Salt	5	mL
	dash	Pepper		dash
1	tsp.	Sugar	5	mL
1	tsp.	Soy sauce	5	mL
2	Tbsp.	Cooking wine	30	mL
1		Egg white	1	
1	Tbsp.	Cornstarch	15	mL
3	Tbsp.	Cooking oil	45	mL
2	slices	Ginger, shredded	2	slices
2	stalks	Green onion, chopped	2	stalks
1		Onion, sliced	1	
2	Tbsp.	Satay sauce	30	mL

1. Wash and dry scallops.
2. Marinate scallops with salt, pepper, sugar, soy sauce, wine, egg white and cornstarch for 20 minutes.
3. Heat cooking oil and stir-fry ginger and green onion. Add scallops and stir-fry in hot wok for 5 minutes. Add sliced onion and continue to stir-fry for another 2 minutes.
4. Add satay sauce. Mix well and toss. Serve hot.

Scallops and Apples

Substitution: shrimp, fish, squid

¾	lb.	Scallops	375	g
½	tsp.	Salt	2	mL
1	Tbsp.	Cooking wine	15	mL
2	Tbsp.	Cooking oil	30	mL
3	small	Apples, cored and sliced	3	small
1		Onion, chopped	1	
¾	cup	Green peas	175	mL
¼	cup	Apple juice	60	mL
2	tsp.	Sugar	10	mL
1	tsp.	Soy sauce	5	mL
1	tsp.	Cornstarch, dissolved in	5	mL
2	Tbsp.	Water	30	mL

1. Marinate scallops with salt and wine.
2. Heat half the cooking oil. Stir-fry apples and onion for 3 minutes. Remove from wok and put aside.
3. Heat remaining cooking oil until very hot. Stir-fry scallops for 5 minutes. Add apples, onion, green peas, apple juice, sugar and soy sauce and cook for another 3 minutes. Thicken with cornstarch solution. Serve hot.

Scallops in Sweet-and-Sour Sauce

A traditional recipe very popular in China.

Substitution: shrimp, fish, oysters

1	lb.	Scallops	500	g
	dash	Salt		dash
2	Tbsp.	Cornstarch	30	mL
		Oil for deep-frying		
3	Tbsp.	Cooking oil	45	mL
4	tsp.	Carrot, shredded and cooked	20	mL
4	tsp.	Fresh mushrooms, sliced	20	mL
4	tsp.	Green pepper, shredded	20	mL
2	tsp.	Vinegar	10	mL
1	tsp.	Salt	5	mL
4	tsp.	Sugar	20	mL
	drops	Sesame seed oil		drops
1	tsp.	Cooking wine	5	mL
1	tsp.	Cornstarch, dissolved in	5	mL
1/4	cup	Water	60	mL

1. Wash scallops and dry with paper towel.
2. Sprinkle scallops with salt and set aside for 5 minutes.
3. Coat scallops with cornstarch. Deep-fry in hot oil for 3 minutes until golden brown. Remove scallops and drain. Discard oil.
4. Heat cooking oil and stir-fry carrot, mushrooms and green pepper for 2 minutes. Add vinegar, salt, sugar, sesame seed oil, scallops and wine. Mix well.
5. Add cornstarch solution and toss well. Serve hot.

Scallops with Pineapple

Substitution: shrimp

1	lb.	Scallops	500	g
4	Tbsp.	Cooking oil	60	mL
½	tsp.	Garlic, minced	2	mL
½	tsp.	Ginger, minced	2	mL
½	cup	Onion, cut into wedges	125	mL
1	cup	Pineapple cubes	250	mL
¼	cup	Green pepper, cut in small squares	60	mL
¼	cup	Red pepper, cut in small squares	60	mL
2	stalks	Green onion, cut into bite-size pieces	2	stalks
¼	tsp.	Salt	1	mL
½	tsp.	Sugar	2	mL
	drops	Sesame seed oil		drops
	dash	Pepper		dash
1	Tbsp.	Cornstarch, dissolved in	15	mL
¼	cup	Water	60	mL

1. Wash and dry scallops.
2. Heat cooking oil. Add scallops and stir-fry for 4 minutes. Remove.
3. Add garlic, ginger and onion. Sauté for 30 seconds, then add scallops, pineapple, green pepper, red pepper, green onion, salt, sugar, sesame seed oil and pepper. Stir-fry for 3 minutes.
4. Add cornstarch solution and bring to a boil. Mix well and place in a hollowed out pineapple to serve.

Fried Squid

1	lb.	Squid	500	g
1	tsp.	Cooking wine	5	mL
½	tsp.	Salt	2	mL
2	slices	Ginger, minced	2	slices
2	stalks	Green onion, finely chopped	2	stalks
¾	cup	Cornstarch	175	mL
		Oil for deep-frying		

1. Clean and score squid and cut crosswise into 2 to 3 pieces. (See "How to Prepare Squid," p. 20.) Cut each piece into narrow strips.
2. Marinate with wine, salt, minced ginger and finely chopped green onion for 20 minutes.
3. Coat with cornstarch.
4. Heat oil and deep-fry squid for about 3 minutes until golden brown. Remove and drain. Place on a plate and serve with any dip, such as sweet-and-sour sauce or plum sauce.

Curried Squid

Substitution: shrimp, oysters, clams

³/₄	lb.	Squid	375	g
1	tsp.	Salt	5	mL
¹/₂	tsp.	Cooking oil	2	mL
1	clove	Garlic, minced	1	clove
2	stalks	Green onion, chopped	2	stalks
1	Tbsp.	Sugar	15	mL
2	Tbsp.	Soy sauce	30	mL
1	tsp.	Curry powder or paste	5	mL
1		Onion, sliced	1	
¹/₄	cup	Carrot, sliced and cooked	60	mL
¹/₄	cup	Green peas	60	mL
¹/₂	cup	Water	125	mL
¹/₄	cup	Milk	60	mL
2	tsp.	Cornstarch, dissolved in	10	mL
¹/₄	cup	Water	60	mL

1. Clean, score and cut squid into small squares. (See "How to Prepare Squid," p. 20.) Sprinkle with salt and set aside.
2. Heat cooking oil. Stir-fry garlic and green onion for 1 minute. Add squid, sugar and soy sauce. Stir-fry for 3 minutes or until squid curls into a roll.
3. Add curry powder, onion, carrot and peas. Stir-fry for 2 minutes.
4. Add water and milk. Cook for 3 minutes. Thicken with cornstarch solution. Serve hot.

Squid with Vegetables

This recipe is ideal for weight-watchers. You can vary the seafood and the vegetables any way you like.

Substitution: oysters, shrimp, clams, fish

¾	lb.	Squid	375	g
	dash	Salt		dash
1	Tbsp.	Cooking wine	15	mL
3	Tbsp.	Cooking oil	45	mL
1	clove	Garlic, minced	1	clove
2	slices	Ginger, minced	2	slices
1	small	Onion, shredded	1	small
½	cup	Mushrooms, sliced	125	mL
½	cup	Carrot, sliced and cooked	125	mL
½	cup	Broccoli flowerets, cooked	125	mL
1	Tbsp.	Soy sauce	15	mL
1	tsp.	Sugar	5	mL
1	tsp.	Salt	5	mL
	dash	Pepper		dash
1	tsp.	Cornstarch, dissolved in	5	mL
3	Tbsp.	Water	45	mL
	drops	Sesame seed oil		drops

1. Clean, score and cut squid into small squares. (See "How to Prepare Squid," p. 20.) Marinate with a dash of salt and wine for 10 minutes.
2. Heat cooking oil. Stir-fry garlic and ginger for 1 minute. Add squid and continue to fry for 3 minutes. Then add onion, mushrooms, carrot, broccoli, soy sauce, sugar, salt and pepper. Stir-fry for another 3 minutes.
3. Add cornstarch solution and sesame seed oil. Bring to a boil. Serve hot.

Squid with Tomatoes

A low-calorie favorite.

Substitution: scallops, fish fillets

1½	lb.	Squid	750	g
	dash	Pepper		dash
1	Tbsp.	Soy sauce	15	mL
1	Tbsp.	Cornstarch	15	mL
3	Tbsp.	Cooking oil	45	ml
2	tsp.	Garlic, minced	10	mL
2	slices	Ginger, shredded	2	slices
2		Tomatoes, peeled, seeded and chopped fine	2	
1	Tbsp.	Tomato paste	15	mL
2	stalks	Green onion, chopped	2	stalks
2	Tbsp.	Cooking wine	30	mL
2	tsp.	Sugar	10	mL
½	tsp.	Salt	2	mL

1. Clean, score and cut squid into small pieces. (See "How to Prepare Squid," p. 20.)
2. Marinate with pepper, soy sauce and cornstarch for 20 minutes.
3. Heat cooking oil. Stir-fry garlic and ginger. Add squid and continue to fry until squid curls. Stir in tomatoes, tomato paste, green onion, wine, sugar and salt. Bring to a boil and simmer for 10 minutes. Serve hot with steamed rice.

Squid with Peppers

Substitution: shrimp, clams

³/₄	lb.	Squid	375	g
		Oil for deep-frying		
2	Tbsp.	Cooking oil	30	mL
2	slices	Ginger, shredded	2	slices
1		Red chili pepper, shredded	1	
1	tsp.	Salt	5	mL
1	Tbsp.	Cooking wine	15	mL
1	Tbsp.	Soy sauce	15	mL
½	tsp.	Pepper	2	mL
1	tsp.	Vinegar	5	mL
¼	tsp.	Sesame seed oil	1	mL
2	stalks	Green onion, chopped	2	stalks

1. Clean, score and cut squid into small squares. (See "How to Prepare Squid," p. 20.)
2. Deep-fry squid for 3 minutes. Remove from oil.
3. Heat cooking oil and stir-fry ginger, red chili pepper and squid. Add salt, wine, soy sauce, pepper and vinegar. Stir-fry for another minute. Add sesame seed oil. Sprinkle with green onion and serve.

Squid in Blackbean Sauce

Substitution: clams, shrimp

¾	lb.	Squid	375	g
½	tsp.	Salt	2	mL
1	Tbsp.	Cooking wine	15	mL
	dash	Pepper		dash
2	tsp.	Salted blackbeans	10	mL
2	tsp.	Garlic, chopped fine	10	mL
2	tsp.	Soy sauce	10	mL
3	Tbsp.	Cooking oil	45	mL
1	tsp.	Ginger, shredded	5	mL
2	stalks	Green onion, shredded	2	stalks
1	tsp.	Red chili pepper, chopped	5	mL
1	tsp.	Sugar	5	mL
1	tsp.	Cornstarch, dissolved in	5	mL
¼	cup	Water	60	mL

1. Clean, score and cut squid into small pieces. (See "How to Prepare Squid," p. 20.)
2. Marinate with salt, wine and pepper.
3. Mash blackbeans and garlic with soy sauce to make a paste.
4. Heat cooking oil. Stir-fry ginger, green onion, red chili pepper, sugar and blackbean paste for 1 minute.
5. Add squid and stir-fry for 5 minutes or until squid curls. Add cornstarch solution. Cook for 2 minutes. Serve hot.

Glossary of Fish and Shellfish

ABALONE is a Pacific shellfish that looks something like a clam, but has a harder and more colorful shell and green meat that is tougher and thicker than clam meat. Its flesh is very delicate and lean.

CLAMS harvested in the Atlantic region are commonly classified as soft-shelled clams or steamers. Hard-shelled clams are less abundant there. The Pacific littleneck clam is harvested mainly in the Strait of Georgia and is usually used as a steamer. Clams are usually gathered along the shoreline at low tide. They have lean flesh and can be used for steaming, pan-frying and in soups.

COD has an elongated body that in the Atlantic species is greyish-green to brownish-red with brown spots. Pacific cod, known as grey cod, is darker on the back than the belly. Harvested throughout the year, cod has lean, white flesh that is easily flaked and is excellent for deep-frying. Often called "the beef of the sea," it is a popular fish in many countries.

CRAB is found along both coasts of North America. In the Atlantic coastal areas it has a smooth reddish shell with dark spots. It is harvested from May through August and is available fresh, frozen or canned. The Pacific Dungeness Crab has clear bulging eyes and a dark brownish-grey color that changes to orange when cooked. It is available all year round, particularly off the west coast of Vancouver Island. Only male crabs that measure 15 cm (6 in.) across the top shell are harvested. The lean white crab flesh is flaky and sweet.

EEL has an elongated body that is black to muddy brown on top and yellowish-white on the belly. It lives in fresh water but breeds at sea. Often called "water snake" because of its length, it has a fatty, firm, white flesh.

FLOUNDER (sole) is one of the most important flat fish caught in the Atlantic. It has both eyes on the top ("eye") side, which is much darker than the blind side. The firm, white, lean flesh is relatively thin and can be deep-fried with the bones. There are basically five kinds of flounder – American plaice, yellowtail flounder, witch flounder, winter flounder and summer flounder – and they are all marketed as sole. They are found in the Gulf of St Lawrence and off the coast of Newfoundland and Labrador.

HADDOCK, long popular on both sides of the Atlantic, is a member of the cod family that ranges in North American waters from the Strait of Belle Isle to Cape Cod. It is harvested inshore, nearshore and offshore by trawls, traps, baited hooks and gillnets all year round. The head and back are greyish-purple and there is a black line on both sides of the body. The underside is silver-grey. The white flesh is lean and tasty and has a soft texture, excellent for smoking and frying.

HAKE is a member of the cod family, with a slender, elongated body and a protruding jaw. The silver hake, commonly called "whiting," has a tasty, firm flesh. The red hake has slender pelvic fins and fewer teeth. Both Atlantic and Pacific species have lean, white flesh and are available fresh, frozen, whole or in fillets.

HALIBUT, found both in the Atlantic and the Pacific, is the largest of the flat fish. It has a large mouth and is dark brown on the eye side and greyish-white on the blind side. It can be caught all year round. Atlantic halibut has firm, white, lean flesh that has made it the highest-priced flat fish in America; Pacific halibut is a medium flat fish. Halibut is available fresh or frozen, in fillets and in steaks. It can be pan-fried or baked.

HERRING, found in lakes and in the Atlantic and Pacific oceans, is a silvery fish with a dark blue or green back and a white abdomen. It has delicate white flesh that is slightly fatty and excellent for deep-frying. It can be smoked, pan-fried and covered with a sauce, pickled or even salted. The Pacific species are important for the production of roe, very popular in Japan. Herring is available frozen, canned, smoked, pickled and salted.

LOBSTER is a popular delicacy throughout the world. Its characteristic huge claws have become the trademark for Atlantic lobster, harvested mostly in the northeastern part of North America. Its shell has a dark green color when fresh, and turns bright red when cooked. It has lean rich flesh and is a colorful ingredient in wok cooking.

MACKEREL has a blue upper surface and silvery-white abdomen. The flesh has an outer band of dark red muscle and an inner portion of lighter meat. Generally considered a fatty fish, mackerel is available whole or in fillet form, fresh, smoked or canned, and is excellent for frying.

MUSSELS, abundant in the Atlantic region, have hard shells with blue-black, brown or black rays. They are gathered from pebbles, rocks and seaweed along the waterline at low tide. The lean flesh is excellent for steaming, stir-frying or soup.

OYSTERS are usually named after the region where they are harvested, as in Blue Point oysters, Cape Cod oysters, and Kent Island oysters. They vary in size and shape. The flesh is lean and rich with a sweet flavor. Considered a delicacy throughout the world, oysters can be eaten raw, pan-fried and deep-fried. They are commonly sold shucked, fresh or frozen. They are often interchangeable with other shellfish in recipes.

PERCH (redfish) has a spiny, orangey-red body and clear black eyes. The flesh is flaky, lean, white and firm, and its distinctive flavor makes it excellent for steaming, poaching whole or pan-frying in a wok. The freshwater variety is yellow perch, and the best is caught in the cold lakes, ponds and streams of Canada's north. Found in both the Atlantic and the Pacific, perch is one of the most important fish caught commercially in the Pacific region. It is available fresh or frozen as fillets.

PICKEREL is a freshwater fish also known as "walleye" or "yellow pike." It has a golden appearance and is considered by many to be one of the best eating fish. Important both as a game fish and a commercial fish, it can be caught all year round. It is a lean fish with white, flaky, firm flesh and a sweet flavor.

NORTHERN PIKE is a freshwater fish sometimes called "jackfish" in North America. Found in lakes, ponds and quiet streams, it is a very popular game fish with white, lean, flaky, firm flesh.

PLAICE is a deep-water fish found in the Atlantic south of Labrador. It is a member of the flounder (sole) family.

POLLOCK, known commercially as "Boston bluefish," looks like cod but has a more rounded body, a projecting lower jaw and a pointed snout. It is caught all year round. A lean, white fish with firm flesh, it is excellent served as fish sticks and fillets.

PRAWNS look like shrimp but are much bigger and have longer feelers and harder shells. They are widely distributed in tropical waters and are a popular delicacy in China. They are grey when raw and pink when cooked. Shrimp can be substituted in most prawn recipes.

REDFISH – See Perch.

RED SNAPPER, caught off the west coast of North America, has a large spiny head, large, clear black eyes and orangey-red skin. The flesh is lean, firm and ideal for fillets.

ROCKFISH is often called "canary rockfish" or "orange rockfish" because of its bright orange color. Harvested all year round along the Pacific coast, it is a lean fish with white, flaky flesh and is excellent for steaming.

SALMON occurs in five species in the Pacific region – pink, sockeye, coho, chum and chinook. They differ in size and shape and the color of the flesh may be white, pink or red. They all have similar nutritional value, although they vary in fat content. The most valuable salmon is the sockeye or red salmon, because of its uniformity of size, its bright red flesh and its high fat content. Next is the popular game salmon, the coho, then the pink salmon, with its delicate pink flesh used mostly for canning; it is a fatty fish with a fine, textured flesh. Chum salmon has pale pink flesh and is often used for canning, salting or freezing. The chinook is a popular sport fish with flesh that varies from red to white. Atlantic salmon has a silvery body with scattered spots. It is classified as a fatty fish. All species can be steamed, pan-fried with sauce, smoked or even served raw, as in sushi.

SCALLOPS are harvested all through the year along the coastal area of the Atlantic region. They are graded by size and shucked as soon as they are caught. The flesh is bone white in color, creamy textured, lean and has a distinctive flavor. It is excellent for stir-frying and deep-frying. It cooks very quickly because it is very sensitive to heat.

SHAD is often mistaken for herring, but is actually much bigger and heavier. It has a dark blue color on top and is sparkling white on the lower sides and abdomen. It is harvested during May and June.

SHRIMP are ten-legged shellfish that are primarily swimmers, as opposed to crab and lobster, which are primarily crawlers with harder shells. Shrimp come in a wide variety of sizes and are grey-green when raw and pink when cooked. They are available fresh, frozen, canned, dried and breaded. Their lean, sweet flesh is excellent for deep-frying. In North America prawns are often also called "shrimp."

SMELT is a small, lean fish that looks like trout and has sweet flesh, a distinctive green top side and a sparkling white abdomen with small dusky spots. It is harvested in Atlantic coastal waters mostly during the fall season. Rainbow smelt, sometimes called American smelt, is found in the Great Lakes. It has a transparent olive to bottle-green back with paler sides and a silvery abdomen. It is a fatty fish with sweet-tasting flesh that is harvested all year round.

SOLE – See Flounder.

SQUID is found along the shores of Newfoundland. Its spotted tubular body has 10 arms and its flesh is lean and white. It can be deep-fried, stir-fried, boiled, baked or steamed.

TROUT is found in lakes and streams and its exterior color ranges from near-black to light green. The flesh is pale ivory to deep pink. Trout is a fatty fish with a distinctive flavor and is excellent for pan-frying or deep-frying.

TUNA varies in flesh color and flavor. The immense Bluefin tuna is the only species readily available in Atlantic waters. It is the largest of the tuna family, with a dark blue upper body and a grey underside. It has a dark fatty muscle and white meat. It is often eaten raw in Japan in sushi and sashimi, and can be substituted for salmon in recipes.

TURBOT, sometimes called "Greenland halibut" or "Newfoundland turbot," is brownish-grey with dark pigmentation and is usually light grey on the underside. Considered a fatty fish, it is suitable for deep-frying and steaming and is often cured or smoked. Although it is sometimes confused with halibut, it is distinctly different, with a higher fat content.

WHITEFISH is caught in the deep waters of the larger lakes in North America, and is the most popular freshwater fish in the world. It belongs to the same family as salmon and trout. Its flesh is white with large flakes and has a delicate sweet flavor, excellent for pan-frying.

INDEX

Photo Credits

Cover: Lobster plate from Mikasa, Wok and Cast Iron Platter from Wok with Yan Restaurant, Cleaver from private collection of Eric Dahlberg; *Seafood Nest:* Deep Fryer from private collection of Eric Dahlberg, Marble from Quadra Stone Co. Ltd.; *Hors d'Oeuvres:* Plate from Mikasa, Slate from Quadra Stone Co. Ltd.; *Sweet and Sour Prawns:* Plate from Mikasa, Steamer from Wok with Yan Restaurant; *Halibut Steaks in Ginger Sauce:* Plate from Quadra Stone Co. Ltd., Cast Iron Platter from Ming Wo Ltd., Cleaver from private collection of Eric Dahlberg; *Crab in Beer Sauce:* Plate from Mikasa; *Squid with Vegetables:* Wok from Wok with Yan Restaurant, Chinese Spatula from private collection of Eric Dahlberg; *Salmon Steaks in Hot Sauce:* Plate from Mikasa, Surface from Chong's Oriental Furniture Centre; *Steamed Whole Snapper in Orange Sauce:* Plate from Quadra Stone Co. Ltd., Steamer from Wok with Yan Restaurant.

Special thanks to: Michael Morisette, Perry Zavitz, Nancy Riesco Marchand and Martha Lowe.